BRINGING THE NCTM STANDARDS TO LIFE:
BEST PRACTICES FROM ELEMENTARY EDUCATORS

Lisa B. Owen
The University of Texas at Austin
Austin, TX

Charles E. Lamb
Texas A & M University
College Station, TX

EYE ON EDUCATION
P.O. BOX 3113
PRINCETON, NJ 08543
(609) 395–0005
(609) 395–1180 fax

ISBN 1-883001-20-X

Library of Congress Cataloging-in-Publication Data

Owen, Lisa B., 1954–
    Bringing the NCTM standards to life : best practices from elementary
educators / by Lisa B. Owen and Charles E. Lamb.
        p.   cm.
    Includes bibliographical references.
    ISBN 1-883001-20-X
    1. Mathematics—Study and teaching (Elementary)—United States.
I. Lamb, Charles E. II. Title.
QA135.5.0938 1996
372.7'044—dc20   96-3195
                                                              CIP

10 9 8 7 6 5 4 3 2 1

Editorial and production services provided by Richard H. Adin Freelance Editorial
Services, 9 Orchard Drive, Gardiner, NY 12525 (914-883-5884)

Innovations in Parent and Family Involvement
by William Rioux and Nancy Berla

The Performance Assessment Handbook
Volume 1: Portfolios and Socratic Seminars
by Bil Johnson

The Performance Assessment Handbook
Volume 2: Performances and Exhibitions
by Bil Johnson

Bringing the NCTM Standards to Life
by Lisa B. Owen and Charles E. Lamb

Mathematics the Write Way
by Marilyn S. Neil

Transforming Education Through Total Quality
Management: A Practitioner's Guide
by Franklin P. Schargel

Quality and Education: Critical Linkages
by Betty L. McCormick

The Educator's Guide to Implementing Outcomes
by William J. Smith

Schools for All Learners: Beyond the Bell Curve
by Renfro C. Manning

TABLE OF CONTENTS

ABOUT THE AUTHORS

Lisa Baughman Owen regularly teaches elementary mathematics methods courses at the University of Texas at Austin. She speaks at regional and national conferences advocating and describing ways of fostering understanding in the elementary mathematics classroom. Dr. Owen is also a former third grade and middle school teacher. She earned her Ph.D. in Curriculum and Instruction at the University of Texas at Austin and an M.S. in Mathematics Education at Florida State University.

Charles E. Lamb received his Ed.D. in Mathematics Education from the University of Georgia. He was a faculty member at the University of Texas at Austin until 1974 when he joined the faculty at Texas A&M University. He teaches graduate and undergraduate courses at the elementary and secondary levels. As an active member of the profession, he is a frequent speaker at professional meetings and often serves as a consultant to schools and other educational agencies.

1

INTRODUCING THE NCTM STANDARDS

INTRODUCTION

John and Terry, high school friends, have summer jobs at a local fruit stand. Mr. Mann, the owner of the fruit stand, showed them how to use the cash register. The register has a scale that weighs the fruit, and then, with the push of a button, it displays the cost of the item on a screen. The two friends eagerly wait on customers, restock fruit, and create fruit displays. One afternoon, while Mr. Mann is away making a delivery, the fruit stand loses electricity.

Just as the power goes off, John sees a customer at the counter with a basket of fruit. The customer wants to buy bananas, apples, and tangerines. The bananas cost 39¢ per pound, the apples cost $1.09 per pound, and the tangerines are 59¢ per pound. John and Terry look at one another. They aren't sure how to handle the situation. John says, "Without any electricity, we'll have to wait for Mr. Mann." Terry sees a scale in the corner of the store and says, "Wait. We can weigh the fruit over there and then figure out the cost on paper."

Once again, they look at each other. They take the fruit over to the scale and put the bananas in first. They blow the dust off the scale to see that there are 3½ pounds of bananas and write down that amount. Then they see there are 2½ pounds of apples and make a note of that amount as well. They measure 4 pounds of tangerines and write down the weight and then walk back over to the counter to figure the cost of the fruit.

John and Terry try to remember the formulas taught to them in school earlier that year. John begins, "I think we learned that when you have fruit problems, you just divide the money by the weight of the fruit. So . . . thirty-nine cents divided by three and a half—that would be point one, one, one, four . . . oh . . . eleven cents."

"No, that can't be right," remarked Terry. "All those bananas for eleven cents? That just doesn't seem like a reasonable answer to me. Maybe we divide the weight of the fruit by the money. Three and a half divided by thirty-nine cents. Oh, eight dollars and ninety-seven cents. That seems better."

"No, now that sounds like too much," says John. "You know, sometimes I see Mr. Mann just telling customers how much their fruit will cost without ever using that cash register. I hear him thinking out loud, first thinking about one pound, then two pounds. Let's look at the problems the way he would look at it."

Terry thinks that is a good idea, so they begin by looking at just the bananas. "Okay," Terry says. "Bananas are thirty-nine cents a pound. If that customer only had one pound, wouldn't it cost just thirty-nine cents?"

John responds, "Oh, yeah! That is just what I hear Mr. Mann saying. So, if one pound costs thirty-nine cents, two pound would be . . . seventy-eight cents."

"Yeah, and three pounds would cost . . . one hundred seventeen cents . . . I mean one dollar and seventeen cents. That want's so hard," remarks Terry.

John is quick to reply, "Okay, but that customer has three and a half pounds of bananas! What would a half a pound cost?"

"That's easy. Half of thirty-nine is . . . hmmmmm." Terry seems stumped.

John has heard Mr. Mann round numbers before. "I think Mr. Mann rounds numbers off when he has an odd number. Why don't we think about rounding thirty-nine to forty, and half of forty is twenty. So, a half a pound of bananas would cost twenty cents. So, let's see . . . to buy all of the bananas, the customer will pay . . . one dollar seventeen cents plus twenty cents equals one dollar and thirty-seven cents."

"Yes, that sounds much more reasonable than our first two answers," says Terry.

John announces, "That wasn't so hard after all . . . and I was going to wait for Mr. Mann to come back. We really can run things while he is away!"

The two finished figuring the cost of the fruit and even remembered to consider sales tax. They were quite proud of themselves at the end of the day and went home smiling.

When John and Terry tried to remember the formulas taught to them in school, they were stumped. They were taught to solve a problem in a particular way and, when they couldn't remember the methods, they almost closed down the fruit stand. Instead, they remembered how Mr. Mann solved the problem, and tried a little problem-solving of their own. They were faced with a real-life problem and worked together to solve it.

Their teachers had told them how to solve problems and gave them "skills." When John and Terry were faced with a situation, they could not fall back on the "skills" because they could not remember them. Fortunately for them, and Mr. Mann, they were able to rely on some problem solving skills they had seen Mr. Mann use.

Unfortunately, John and Terry's teachers have used instructional techniques revolving around the teaching of minimum skills. It is curious that John and Terry often found themselves with low grades even though they are quite talented in their problem solving abilities. They were able to think through their fruit stand problem and work cooperatively to solve it. In school, they were never given the opportunity to show what they knew. They were given work sheets to complete paper and pencil tests on Fridays.

The present educational system, which promotes instruction of minimum skills, is a ". . . product of the industrial age" (National Council of Teachers of Mathematics (NCTM), 1989, p. 3). News reports have made it common knowledge that elementary students are not experiencing success with mathematics. In 1989, the authors of the *Curriculum and Evaluation Standards for School Mathematics* (NCTM, 1989) expressed concern for the mathematical welfare of this country's children and offered curriculum standards to promote change in learning and teaching; the goal was to develop mathematical power for all students. Two years later, the *Professional Standards for Teaching Mathematics* (NCTM, 1991) was published. The *Professional Standards* was intended to aid teachers in the shift from a traditional mode of instruction to a more current mode — to empower students — to develop the kind of teaching that would turn the mathematics classroom into a mathematical community. One concern, as mathematical communities developed in the classroom, became that teachers would need to find new ways to assess student progress and understanding. The *Assessment Standards for School Mathematics* (NCTM, 1995) was designed to study student performance — what the student understands and how the student investigates, questions, and faces problems. Central to the *Assessment Standards* (NCTM, 1995), ". . . is that decisions regarding students' achievement should be made on the basis of a convergence of information from a variety of balanced and equitable sources" (p. 1).

The *Curriculum and Evaluation Standards* stresses curricular reform and contends that students must actively create knowledge. The notion that students can passively absorb information is unacceptable. The *Curriculum and Evaluation Standards* has not only made educators and researchers aware of the need for change, it has also provided some direction for change in learning and teaching. The *Curriculum and Evaluation Standards* begins with a set of goals:

> . . . [T]hat students should be exposed to numerous and varied interrelated experiences that encourage them to value the mathematical enterprise, to develop mathematical habits of mind, and to understand and appreciate the role of mathematics. . . . (p. 5)

Various strategies for teaching mathematics have been attempted. Lecture and an emphasis on rote memorization are falling by the wayside. Teachers are fostering an understanding of mathematics by developing an autonomous environment. Students are responsible for the search for solutions and teachers are compelling students to talk openly and freely about their ideas and solutions.

Mathematics educators and researchers suggest an activity-oriented classroom. In an activity-oriented classroom the teacher promotes reasoning and encourages children to exchange viewpoints which foster confidence in students' abilities to think (Kamii & Joseph, 1989). As students discuss and exchange viewpoints a shift occurs in the locus of authority (Schifter & Fosnot, 1993). There is no longer one right answer and the classroom becomes a "community of inquiry" (p. 11). In a community of inquiry, teachers are able to promote reasoning and sense-making (NCTM, 1989). Instruction in an activity-oriented classroom should incorporate a variety of activities which include the manipulation of materials and the opportunity for discussion and interaction. The teacher should not only provide opportunities for individual work, but should also include opportunities for cooperative learning. If students are to learn, they need to reflect on their own thoughts, as well as the thoughts and ideas of others.

To provide an activity-oriented environment teachers will have to follow a set of standards, the *Professional Standards* (NCTM, 1991). A framework has been organized, within the *Professional Standards*, that emphasizes the decisions a teacher needs to make concerning instruction. The teacher needs to select or create worthwhile mathematical tasks, tasks that engage students' interest and intellect, as well as stimulate them to problem-solve and make connections between mathematical ideas. Communication plays a major role in developing this mathematical community. The teacher needs to promote interactions among students, interactions that will promote and challenge their thinking.

In the few, short years since *Curriculum and Evaluation Standards* was published, innovations in the teaching of mathematics have occurred across the country. Although a variety of innovative teaching practices are described in this book, the practices share one primary commonality — the children, in each case, are actively involved in the learning process. They are actively involved, either mentally or physically or both. This is an illustration of constructivism — not a new learning theory, but one whose influence has increased in the past decade.

CONSTRUCTIVISM

Many researchers in mathematics education have offered interpretations of constructivism and there are, therefore, varying perspectives on the topic. All share the notion that the learner takes ownership for learning and that knowledge is actively constructed by the individual.

Ernst von Glasersfeld (1990) calls Jean Piaget the "great pioneer of the constructivist theory of knowing" (p. 22). He summarizes Piaget's beliefs and contends, "Knowledge is not passively received either through the senses or by way of communication. Knowledge is actively built up by the cognizing subject" (p. 22). von Glasersfeld reminds the reader that a shift to mathematical constructivism is not an easy task; the traditional ways of teaching are slow to disappear and at times lie dormant and can quietly return. von Glasersfeld emphasizes that a theory of knowing is the responsibility of the knower.

Given that knowing is the responsibility of the knower, a constructivist teacher would acknowledge that children interpret not only individual work in different ways but also interpret instructional situations differently (Yackel, Cobb, Wood, & Merkel, 1990). Yackel, Cobb, Wood, and Merkel contend that learning is based on children's experiences in the classroom and occurs as children build mathematical meaning based on those experiences. Yackel and his colleagues support the need to insure that children construct mathematical knowledge in ways that make it personally meaningful.

Understanding mathematics comes from the view that learning is basically a process of concept construction and active interpretation instead of the absorption and accumulation of collected pieces of information (Schifter & Fosnot, 1993). Schifter and Fosnot emphasize that the creation of mathematical understanding is the product of interpretive and constructive activity. These authors suggest that, for many teachers, conceptions of mathematics are based on giving specific explanations resulting in getting the right answers. If interpreting and constructing promote understanding, then teachers must come to understand that explaining will not be enough because they are not able to understand for their students. Therefore, the student must be given the latitude to work alone and/or with others to explore, examine, and investigate objects or ideas.

According to Clements and Battista (1990), a constructivist is one who believes that knowledge is not passively received but actively created by the child. New mathematical knowledge is created by reflecting on mental and physical actions. The constructivist believes that mathematical interpretations are molded by experience and social interaction. Children learn through a social process in a culture, a classroom culture, which involves discovery, invention, negotiation, sharing, and evaluation (Clements & Battista, 1990).

The key word in all of these descriptions is active; active in the physical sense, possibly, but more importantly, active in the mental sense. There must be some consideration, or reflection, of a problem for the construction of knowledge to occur. Descriptors of this experience could be: apply, examine, interact, interpret, judge, negotiate, prove, and/or represent. It is through these actions that children are able to make sense of mathematics.

LEARNING MATHEMATICS

There are two basic questions to be asked ask if we want children to learn mathematics: What will children need to do? and What will teachers need to do? What children do will be dependent upon the actions of the teacher.

To promote the child's construction of mathematical knowledge, the teacher's role should be one of facilitator. The teacher will need to recognize that children require some type of conflict (Ginsburg & Opper, 1988) if construction of new knowledge is to take place. Learning mathematics can be considered an active problem-solving process as children are faced with a conflict. The teacher, as facilitator, must be able to provide problem situations and promote reasoning and investigating. The teacher must also encourage interactions and provide an environment conducive to students asking questions and solving problems. When problem-solving situations are provided, children interact, reason, investigate; they construct knowledge (Yackel, Cobb, Wood, Wheatley, & Merkel, 1990).

As the teacher works to provide a problem-solving environment for the students, an additional question arises, a question of how we think about mathematics: What should the study of mathematics entail? This question can best be answered by examining the *Curriculum and Evaluation Standards* (NCTM, 1989).

THE *CURRICULUM AND EVALUATION STANDARDS*: GRADES KINDERGARTEN THROUGH 4

The first four standards in the *Curriculum and Evaluation Standards*, whether looking at grades K–4, 5–8, or 9–12, are the same:

- Standard 1: Mathematics as Problem Solving
- Standard 2: Mathematics as Communication
- Standard 3: Mathematics as Reasoning
- Standard 4: Mathematical Connections

There is a reason *Mathematics as Problem Solving* is the first of these standards. The authors of the *Curriculum and Evaluation Standards* believe, "Problem solving should be the central focus of the mathematics curriculum" (p. 23). The authors also believe that children learn concepts and skills when teachers provide a problem-solving approach to instruction. If what is to be learned is embedded in a problem situation, children will think, question, talk, and, in other words, find some way to make sense of the information. This sense-making process is how they come to understand the information.

The second, third, and fourth standards are key elements in this sense-making process. "Communication plays an important role in helping children construct links between their informal, intuitive notions and the abstract language and symbolism of mathematics" (p. 26). *Standard 2: Mathematics as Communication* stresses the importance of children talking and listening. It is through this discourse that children learn the language of mathematics and they learn about their thinking when they listen to themselves. When given opportunities to talk, children are able to clarify their thoughts as well as learn of other children's perspectives. It is at this point that they may come to realize that there is more than one way to solve a problem. If teachers convince children to justify their thinking and push children to defend their solutions then children will be in a better position to develop mathematical reasoning.

Standard 3: Mathematics as Reasoning promotes the development of an environment that "places critical thinking at the heart of instruction" (p. 29). Within this environment teachers and students should feel free to discuss and argue their points of view. As they look at each others' perspectives they are having to justify their own thoughts in the process — they are making sense of new information — they are reasoning.

In the traditional classroom setting, children often learn mathematics one topic at a time. When they learn one topic at a time, they see mathematics as a series of isolated topics, they aren't given an opportunity to make connections. *Standard 4: Mathematical Connections* moves away from that notion by encouraging children to see the relationships between mathematical ideas. Teachers can help children see relationships between mathematical ideas, between mathematics and real-world situations, between mathematics and other school subjects. When children make these connections mathematics becomes much more than computation, it becomes real, something with a purpose.

The remaining standards reflect concepts. The importance of

problem-solving, communication, reasoning, and making connections can be found within each of the remaining standards. In grades Kindergarten through 4, the *Curriculum and Evaluation Standards* addresses estimation, number sense and numeration, concepts of whole number operations, whole number computation, geometry and spatial sense, measurement, statistics and probability, fractions and decimals, and patterns and relationships.

The Kindergarten through 4th grade curriculum should include estimation (Standard 5). Using words such as closer to, about, and between lets children know that they don't always have to be exact in their answers. Teachers use this vocabulary every day: "Whoever is **closest** to the lights, please turn them off when the film begins." "You have **about** 10 more minutes of recess." "We will meet in the area **between** the swings and the parking lot." If teachers directed students' attention toward the vocabulary, students would be in a better position to make the connection to the notion that being exact isn't always necessary.

Children should be involved in a variety of activities that help them discern when it is appropriate to estimate and when an exact answer is necessary: Do you need to know how much your backpack weighs, or is it enough to know it is light enough to carry all the way home? Do you need to know exactly how much money is in your pocket before you go to the checkout counter to buy candy, or is your estimate good enough? If students begin estimation at an early age, then accepting estimation "as a legitimate part of mathematics" should feel natural to them.

When children enter school, many are able to add and count and to use counting to solve a variety of arithmetic problems. They have already developed some number sense. They model problems and invent procedures when computing answers (Carpenter, 1985). When teachers discourage invented procedures and require students to solve problems in a set, systematic manner, children begin to make a tradeoff. They trade their inventive, problem-solving methods for mechanical applications of arithmetic skills (Carpenter, 1985; Resnick, 1987). Soon, they are only interested in getting the "right answer."

Most young children have some sense of number — show any 4-year-old two plates of cookies, one with two cookies on it, the other with five, then ask if he/she would rather have two cookies or five. The child will show you he/she knows about quantity. If teachers incorporate real-world experiences into instruction as they help children develop number sense and numeration (Standard 6), then children will be able to make connections to previous experiences.

Teachers should give children opportunities to compare number and quantity, to count, and to explore number relationships with physical materials. Students should be actively involved in classroom discussions and should be prompted to use their own language so that these connections will be easier (and more comfortable) for them to make and accept.

As children develop number sense and compare quantities, they may also be looking at concepts of whole number operations (Standard 7).

> One essential component of what it means to understand an operation is recognizing conditions in real-world situations that indicate that the operation would be useful in those situations. Other components include building an awareness of models and the properties of an operation, seeing relationships among operations, and acquiring insight into the effects of an operation of a pair of numbers. (p. 41)

Teachers should introduce a variety of problems within the context of real-world situations. These problems should provide children with informal experiences that will develop the understanding needed before beginning instruction or discussion of computation. The comparing of cookies could be used, once again. Ask the child if he/she wants two cookies or five cookies. When the teacher hears the answer "five" the next question can be, "Why would you rather have five?" The child may say, "Because five is more than two." The teacher could ask, "How many more is five than two?" This is an example of providing students with a dilemma, asking for a solution, and asking them to reason. The student begins to develop some concept of whole number operations, in this case, subtraction.

The instruction of whole number computation (Standard 8) takes on many forms. This standard promotes the use of calculators as one component of instruction. By incorporating calculators into instruction students will develop thinking strategies, recognize the reasonableness of answers, attain self-confidence, and acknowledge how time can be used more efficiently. This standard also advocates the notion that there are can be more than one way to solve a problem.

Students often find different ways to solve problems, to compute answers. Teachers are now accepting the notion that there might be more than one way to solve a problem. In the past, children who answered correctly but worked the algorithm incorrectly may have felt scolded when they heard, "No, that is not the way we subtract." By providing opportunity for discussion, teachers are hearing a variety of solutions to problems. Some children, when given the problem 74 minus 19 might change the problem to 75 minus 20, some may change the problem to 70 minus 20 plus 5, while others may regroup and solve in a more traditional manner. A discussion of the strategies will prove quite enlightening to the students and the teacher.

Geometry and spatial sense (Standard 9) is another important aspect of the elementary mathematics curriculum. "Geometry helps us represent and describe in an orderly manner the world in which we live" (p. 48). Children must explore and investigate with everyday objects as well as with shapes. These investigations will help them see connections between the shapes and the everyday objects they are exploring. Children may look at the classroom clock and see a circle, the face of their book and see a rectangle, the tile on the floor and see a square, an orange cone or a ball at recess and see a cone or a sphere, a can in the cafeteria and see a cylinder. As they explore they learn about the properties of objects as well as develop an awareness of spatial concepts, and it is the teacher that can help guide these observations.

Children often wonder why a particular topic is useful. Measurement (Standard 10) is one topic that can help children see just how useful mathematics is in everyday life. Measurement can also be considered a springboard for exploring operations as well as fractions and decimals. The work should begin at an informal level — have children look at two rocks, which is heavier? Give them a stick then have them draw a line that is longer than the stick. At this stage, children consider attributes and make comparisons. Before formal use of measurement tools begins, children should have many of these experiences as well as experiences using nonstandard units of measurement. They can compare lengths of paper taped to the floor using paper clips or their feet; the choice is arbitrary. "Children can see the usefulness of measurement if classroom experiences focus on measuring real objects, making objects of given sizes, and estimating measurements" (p. 53). If the goal is for children to relate these experiences to real-world situations, then they will need to actually make measurements in their classroom, in the school, and at home.

Children spend a great deal of time collecting and organizing materials. The study of statistics and probability (Standard 11) promotes the collecting, organizing, and describing of data, interpreting of graphs, and exploring concepts of chance. These identifiers all conjure up the activity-oriented classroom. The teacher can produce a variety of activities that will develop these skills by using classroom materials, food preferences, or the newspaper (weather, sports, fashion trends, population). The teacher can promote discussion by getting children to talk about their favorite ice cream, musician, or television show. Graphs can be made that illustrate the information and which can aid in the discussion of interpreting and comparing data.

The class can discuss the probability of teams winning and losing; they can study the statistics of past games to help make their predictions. They can also consider weather conditions: Will they need to wear raincoats to school the next day? Can they plan an outdoor picnic for the first part of January — why or why not? The study of statistics and probability can undoubtedly promote thought and discussion.

In the early grades, children need a variety of experiences that will help them develop concepts and number sense of fractions and decimals (Standard 12). The teacher must first think about how fractions might be useful in everyday life; sharing food with other children is often a good way to begin a discussion. Slicing apples and pizzas are good ways to talk about fractions since the teacher can choose which way to divide the material — in halves, thirds, fourths.

Oral language is most important for beginning instruction. Students must see, hear, and talk about dividing pizzas and apples and candy bars into equal parts. By spending time on and emphasizing basic ideas, it has been found that the time currently spent in the upper grades, "correcting students' misconceptions and procedural difficulties," (p. 57) can be greatly reduced; therefore, discussion, use of the language, and use of materials should be plentiful before symbols are introduced, for fractions as well as decimals.

Looking for patterns and relationships (Standard 13) can be continual. Children will be able to discover patterns in the classroom (all desks in groups of five), in the halls (a blue floor tile, two white floor tiles, a blue tile, two white tiles), at home (in the fabric on a chair), and anyplace they choose to wander (windows on a building, fence posts). These patterns and relationships will be found in a variety of forms including, but not limited to, shapes and numbers.

> From the earliest grades, the curriculum should give students opportunities to focus on regularities in events, shapes, designs, and sets of numbers. Children should begin to see that regularity is the essence of mathematics. (p. 60)

Teachers should encourage children to explore the patterns all around them. Then they can come back to the classroom to identify properties, make comparisons, and make connections.

The *Curriculum and Evaluation Standards* provides many models for students' learning. The intent is to develop that mathematical power in all students by providing students with as much exposure to mathematical ideas as possible. By approaching students with a variety of problem-solving situations that require them to think and reason as well as talk about their thinking, learning will take place.

What kinds of problem-solving situations will be appropriate for the students? The teacher will need to find problems that engage the students. The tasks the teacher assigns must seem worthwhile to the students or the problems will not be completed — at least not with any real enthusiasm or zest for learning. The *Professional Standards* is a guide teachers can use to help them develop an environment conducive to thinking and learning.

THE *PROFESSIONAL STANDARDS FOR TEACHING MATHEMATICS*

There are six teaching standards in the *Professional Standards for Teaching Mathematics*. The *Professional Standards* focuses on what the teacher must do to create an environment necessary for constructing meaning. All six of the standards are needed if the children are to thrive in the classroom.

Planning Worthwhile Mathematical Tasks is the first of the six teaching standards. Teachers should provide tasks that develop mathematical thinking, that captivate and challenge a student's intellect. The teacher must decide, when selecting a task, how appropriately the task represents the concepts to be learned, as well as how the task corresponds to a student's prior knowledge and experiences.

It is, therefore, the teacher's role to learn about the students' interests and experiences. It might be valuable to find out what the students do after school — are they involved in scouts, sports, dance? Equally valuable is for the teacher to set aside time to watch the popular television shows, look at current magazines, and play the favored video and computer games. The main ideas of the shows and games can be integrated into word problems and discussions. Students will also observe the teacher's interest in the their world which should give them a feeling of value.

The *Teacher's Role in Discourse* (Standard 2) states that teachers should facilitate discourse by first posing challenging questions, then by listening to students' responses/ideas. The teacher must promote interactions in the classroom that will enable students to clarify ideas, either verbally or on paper.

It is sometimes difficult for a teacher to stand back when a student is puzzled over a problem, but this is the time that the student is really trying to make sense of the problem. Instead of telling the student how to solve the problem, the teacher should ask a question that will get the student to think out loud — the point being to continue to listen as the student comes to terms with the dilemma. This is a time to assess the student's understanding — what is the problem asking, what is the student's plan?

The teacher must also find ways to get students to listen; to listen to each other as well as the teacher. The *Students' Role in Discourse* (Standard 3) promotes the facilitation of student discourse as a means for exploration. When students talk about problems and solutions they are better able to make sense of the tasks that teachers provide.

Often, all it takes is posing a question: a student raises his hand, asks a question, then immediately says, "Oh never mind, now I see!" Having the opportunity to listen to oneself can be all that is necessary to understand. There might be a time when a peer is better able to explain a problem or solution. A teacher may spend 20 minutes explaining a procedure and look out to see some blank faces, then a student comes to the front of the room and says, "The way I see it. . . ." The next sound to be heard is another student saying, "Oh, now I get it!" Students must encounter a variety of perspectives and perceptions that come from themselves, each other, and their teacher.

There will be times when manipulatives will be the best mode for promoting mathematical thinking. This is what drives the fourth standard, *Tools for Enhancing Discourse*. The tools teachers can provide may range from paper and pencil for drawing or graphing, to calculators, to dice, to blocks. Any material that can help the student envision his/her thinking and then be able to explain that thinking to the class will be beneficial.

Another tool to consider is literature. To begin a discussion on number sense, the teacher might read the poem "Smart" by Shel Silverstein (1974). The poem provides a humorous look at how a child understands money. He is very excited and proud of the dollar bill his father gives him. He is so excited he trades the dollar for two quarters, then trades the two quarters for three dimes. He exchanges the three dimes for four nickels and in the end has five pennies. He seems more excited than ever because he knows that, "five is more than four." The poem ends with the child thinking that his father is really proud of his dealings because of the way his father looks at him. The poem and the description of the father's looks would be humorous to anyone with an understanding of numbers.

Looking at how students respond to the poem will provide the teacher with an idea about the students' understanding of numbers and money. After that initial survey, the teacher can ask questions: "What did you think about the boy's actions?" "How much money did he start with?" How much money did he have at the end of the poem?" "What happened during the course of this poem?" Poems and children's books can often promote discourse to explore and then extend children's mathematical notions.

For a classroom filled with teacher and student discourse to evolve, the teacher will need to pay attention to the *Learning Environment* (Standard 5). The environment will be key to the teacher's success. If the students are comfortable and secure in the classroom, they will feel free to take risks, to talk about their own ideas — even when they believe their ideas are obscure.

The teacher will need to create this environment beginning the first day of school. The students must know that mistakes are accepted and perhaps encouraged. The teacher could challenge students to say anything they are thinking, no matter how strange or insignificant they might believe their ideas to be, then the teacher could applaud them for making a contribution. The teacher must also let it be known that teasing or snickering will not be tolerated.

The final teaching standard, *Analysis of Teaching and Learning*, addresses the importance of assessment. Teachers gather information about each student to get grades but there are many other reasons for assessment. The gathering of information should be considered an ongoing analysis of the learning that takes place. Through that analysis the teacher can also assess his/her own teaching practices. The teacher may ask:

Is everyone learning solid, meaningful mathematics?

Am I providing challenges to my students?

Do I need to make any changes during instruction or to subsequent lessons?

Do I have enough information to talk about a student's learning to the student and possibly to his/her parents.

There are a variety of ways to assess student learning. The National Council of Teachers of Mathematics believes assessment to be of such importance that they published a new book of standards, the *Assessment Standards for School Mathematics* (NCTM, 1995). This book is addressed in the next section.

THE *ASSESSMENT STANDARDS FOR SCHOOL MATHEMATICS*

One major concern for teachers is assessment. Students' test scores don't always reflect their understanding of concepts. As innovative practices infiltrate the elementary mathematics classroom, a ripple effect is being observed. In the beginning, the outcomes of innovative teaching practices didn't match assessment. Therefore, a common complaint was, "Students are more actively involved in the learning process, they are problem-solving, and certainly seem to understand, but when it comes to assessment they are not making the grade. What do we need to do differently?"

Because of low test scores, some teachers revert back to more traditional practices, but many continue their innovative ideas. Whether these innovations are due to the *Curriculum and Evaluation Standards*, the *Professional Standards*, or an enthusiasm in teaching for understanding, methods of assessment are changing.

The authors of the *Assessment Standards* (1995) state that many of the items on current tests are "uninteresting and superficial." They feel that assessment should concentrate on the mathematics that is most significant for children to learn. The authors have broken down the assessment process into four interrelated phases, and believe that the phases ". . . can be characterized by the decisions and actions that occur during them" (p. 4). An assessor begins by planning the assessment and must decide what purpose the assessment will serve, what methods will be used for collecting and interpreting evidence, what criteria will be used for evaluating performances on activities, and what formats will be used for summarizing judgements and reporting results. Then the assessor gathers evidence and must look at how activities and tasks will be developed or chosen, how these activities and tasks will be selected for engaging students, and how methods for developing and maintaining evidence of the actions will be judged. The assessor must also interpret the evidence and examine how the quality of the evidence will be determined, how an understanding of the actions of students will be determined from the evidence, look at the specific criteria that will be used to assess the actions as well as insure that the criteria were implemented in an appropriate manner, and decide how the interpretations of the actions will be summarized as results. The assessor must decide how to use the results, what ways will the results be recounted, how will the assessor draw conclusions, what decisions will be made based on those conclusions, and decide how these results will be used in further instruction and assessment. The assessor might make decisions about one of the phases while in the middle of another. While interpreting the evidence, the assessor may realize a need to gather more evidence or make a new plan for assessment. These phases, ". . . should serve as markers to be used as a guide" (p. 4).

Six assessment standards have been developed that embody a new criteria for appraising the suitableness of mathematics assessment practices. The goal is to build new assessment systems that reflect the changes in place because of the efforts of NCTM.

The first standard (the *Mathematics Standard*), "Assessment should reflect the mathematics that all students need to know and be able to do," focuses on the mathematical power that students should possess. A student's mathematical power is assessed as he/she solves problems, makes connections from one mathematical idea to another, reasons, and makes conclusions or inferences. The student may also engage in mathematical problem-solving by using a computer or calculator or any other tools that may be available. Factual knowledge as well as skills may also be assessed as the student formulates or solves a problem. These skills should be considered ". . . in the same way they are used, as tools for performing mathematically significant tasks" (p. 11).

Growing out of the notion that students continue learning as they are being assessed is the second standard (the *Learning Standard*), "Assessment should enhance mathematics learning." When students are engaged in discussion, they are thinking out loud and making sense of their own ideas. The teacher can tell, by listening, what they understand and don't understand. A back and forth discussion can help students clarify their thoughts and build understanding.

Lessons and activities don't have to stop so the teacher can give the students some kind of formal assessment; and when students are given a formal assessment, if the assessment does not match what they have been doing in the classroom, the students are quick to realize what is important and what is not important (and it is not the activities). "Assessment does not simply mark the end of a learning cycle. Rather, it is an integral part of instruction that encourages and supports further learning" (p. 13). Informal assessments can be ongoing, whether through observation, conferences, or listening to how children make sense of information during class discussions.

Also, with ongoing assessment, students begin to reflect on their work, as they work. Teachers can help students become more independent, to become self-assessors by explaining how tasks and criteria were developed, and by demonstrating how the criteria are applied. The teacher must make certain that the assessment will match what is going on in the classroom, that the students can transfer what they already know to new situations, as well as help students develop confidence and independence.

What is wonderful about the third standard (the *Equity Standard*),

"Assessment should promote equity," is that students can show off what they know. They can be pinpointed for their own contributions, their own ideas, their uniqueness. The assessment process must allow for these differences. "Assessment is equitable when students with special needs or talents have access to the same accommodations and modifications they receive in instruction" (p. 15).

With teachers and students bringing different perspectives to the classroom, teachers will need to be more informed about the values and norms of racial, ethnic, gender, cultural, and social groups. Teachers must also realize that students may be members of more than one group, therefore, stereotyping is inconceivable.

The issue of equity is complex. In the past, assessments have ignored differences and some students have been left out; some have not been given the same opportunities for learning. Students have also been left out because assessments were not designed to enhance mathematics learning or aid in the continuation of learning. If the teacher considers students' backgrounds and experiences, and promotes each student's best work, then their self-esteem and confidence will build. They will be eager to learn, eager to show what they know.

The *Openness Standard*, "Assessment should be an open process," is the fourth standard. Students need to know what they will be learning, how they will be assessed, and the significance of the assessment. "When students understand the criteria used in judging their work and are shown examples of adequate and inadequate responses, their performance improves" (p. 17). Not only should students be informed but also parents, administrators, policymakers, and any others interested in the process.

In an open assessment process, teachers meet with other teachers to consider learning goals. They may also address how they will assess those goals and find ways to report results. Since assessment is an ongoing process, opportunity for modifying the assessment process can also be ongoing. Teachers can examine an assessment's effectiveness and revise in any way that seems appropriate.

Teachers must make certain that students are aware of the process, as well as the consequences, of assessment. Also, by providing appropriate tasks and keeping students informed, not only will students have a better idea of what they are learning, but the teachers will also be able to tell if the assessment is appropriate or if it needs some modification.

What kind of information will teachers receive from the assessment? The fifth standard (the *Inference Standard*), "Assessment should promote valid inferences about mathematics learning," should be considered a guide to gaining valid information. Teachers make inferences based on the assessment and "An inference about learning is a conclusion about a student's cognitive processes that cannot be observed directly. The conclusion has to be based instead on the student's performance" (p. 19). Observing, planning conferences, providing open-ended tasks, and using portfolios will all help tell a story about the student's performance.

To tell a clear story of a student's performance or to be able to read and understand another educator's description of a student's performance, the sixth standard (the *Coherence Standard*), "Assessment should be a coherent process," comes into play. Educators must make certain that:

+ The assessment process forms a coherent whole; the phases fit together.
+ The assessment matches the purposes for which it is being done.
+ The assessment is aligned with the curriculum and with instruction. A student's learning connects with their assessment experiences. (p. 21)

The coherence standard is intended to emphasize the importance of the need for balance in the assessment process. In the past, teachers have assigned grades to students based on paper and pencil tests or worksheets alone. The paper and pencil tests can't give an accurate picture of all students when the diversity of the students is considered. Instead, a balance among the varying activities and forms of assessments will help all children learn and give a better picture of their understanding and knowledge. Maintaining this balance also means that the assessment must correspond with the aim of the activity. The teacher's job is a full one; the assessment activities must have a purpose, they must make sense to the students (based on cultural, gender, ethnic, racial, social differences), and they must vary in order to get a true picture of each student's knowledge and perceptions.

What the *Assessment Standards* proposes is to use assessment as a tool — a tool to collect evidence about a student's understanding, knowledge, and use of mathematics, as well as the student's disposition towards mathematics. Once that information is attained, it can be used to consider students' progress for numerous educational purposes. Teaching, learning, and assessing the function of the teacher are being revitalized as the *Curriculum and Evaluation, Professional,* and *Assessment Standards* come together.

WHAT WE PRESENT

In this book, you will find profiles of 13 educators. Their stories embody the goings on in their classrooms or school environments. These educators are all familiar with the *Curriculum and Evaluation Standards,* but some were engaged in their standard-like thinking, planning, and teaching before the *Curriculum and Evaluation Standards* were published. Those educators were pleased to have their ideas validated by the National Council of Teachers of Mathematics.

The subjects of this book live and work in various locations across the United States. Chapter 2 consists of 12 of the profiles, descriptions of the educators and their actions. These descriptions are based on surveys and interviews. A discussion following each profile looks at connections between the educator's actions and the *Curriculum and Evaluation Standards,* the *Professional Standards,* and the *Assessment Standards.*

Chapter 3 is devoted to the profile of one 1st grade teacher. This teacher created a unit that encompassed all three *Standards.* We felt an in-depth study of the actions of that teacher was in order.

Chapter 4 addresses the characteristics of the educators' actions. The initial questions: "What will children need to do to learn mathematics?" "What will teachers need to do?" and "What should the study of mathematics entail?" will be revisited. Some additional questions to be considered include, "Do any characteristics continually emerge?" and "Can the activities described in this book be incorporated into instruction in other elementary classrooms?" We hope you will find connections, as well as an approach that can be implemented in your classroom, school, or district.

2

BEST PRACTICES

THE CHESS TOURNAMENT

The students in two 4th grade classrooms, classroom 101 and 102 wanted to learn to play chess. They decided that once they knew knew how to play the game they would have a tournament. The teachers in the two classrooms developed their units, and decided they would spend 45 minutes each day for 2 weeks preparing for the tournament.

The teacher in classroom 101 began by telling the students what they would learn. The students would learn the names of the pieces, how the pieces were positioned on the board, and how each piece could be moved on the board. For example, on the first day the teacher described the king and queen then told the students that the king and queen always occupied the two central squares on the first row. The teacher showed them the two pieces, named the pieces, and had the students repeat the names. The teacher displayed an overhead that showed the placement of the pieces. Then the teacher reviewed — what were the names of the chess pieces being held up in front of the class? In what position were the two pieces placed on the board? The teacher called on all students, asking each to come up to the overhead to appropriately place the two pieces for all to observe. The teacher followed this plan for all the pieces. On day two, the students learned about the rook and the bishop, on day three the knight and the pawn, and on day four they reviewed the names and positions of all the pieces.

The teacher began day five by telling students how the pieces could only move in certain directions, beginning with the ways they could move the king and queen. These movements were then displayed on the overhead. The students then had to repeat what they knew about the direction of the movement. This method of instruction was followed for days six, seven, and eight with the other chess pieces.

There were two days of instruction left before the tournament would begin. It was time to talk about the rules of the game as well as the ultimate goal — capturing your opponent's king. Day nine was spent in discussion and on the last day the teacher distributed game boards and pieces to the students so they could practice the game.

The teacher in classroom 102 wrote a different unit. The students needed to know the names of the pieces, but the teacher wanted to make sure that the students developed strategies for capturing the king. Before the lessons began, the teacher made a poster. The poster consisted of a key that showed and named the chess pieces, as well as included a drawing of a chess board. On the drawing of the board were labels of the pieces to show their placement and in another picture were the pieces with arrows drawn to show their movement.

On the first day the teacher distributed chess boards and chess pieces to groups of four students. The teacher reminded the students that they had wanted to learn to play chess and each day, for 2 weeks, they would have a chance to learn and practice before the tournament. The teacher showed them the poster, named the pieces, and told the students that each piece had a special position on the board, as well as a certain task. The teacher then distributed a copy of the poster to each group and said, "This is a time for exploration." The students played with the board and the pieces for the remainder of the first day.

On the second day, the teacher began by asking if anyone had ever played soccer. Students began relaying stories, telling their favorite part of playing — trying to block the ball from the goal, trying to make a goal, trying to take the ball away from an opponent. The teacher asked what it meant to play offensively and defensively. Once they talked about playing the game of soccer, the teacher helped them make a connection to chess. The goal of chess was to capture the king, the goal of soccer was to accumulate points by kicking the ball into the net; how you reached either goal took offensive and defensive moves. As the teacher talked about soccer players and their responsibilities on the field, the connection was made to the chess pieces and how the pieces moved on a chess board, and the teacher reminded them, once again, of the goals of the games. There wasn't much time left for day two. The teacher told them to think about how they liked playing soccer, offensively and defensively, and then reminded them of the poster showing how the pawn, bishop, and rook could move on the board. The students took turns, two students against two students, moving their pieces for the remainder of the second day; the teacher was free to listen and observe the students' movements.

The teacher decided to begin the third day of instruction with some questions: "Did you think about soccer or chess and how you liked playing — offensively or defensively? Can you think of any other games where you might play offensively or defensively?" The questions were designed to get the students thinking about the role they might undertake when playing chess or any of the other games they discussed. As they discussed games, Checkers and Tic-Tac-Toe came into the discussion first. Some students talked about how they liked taking the lead early then pushing on to win, while others liked chasing after their opponents, blocking their every move.

This was a good time to take up the discussion on chess. The teacher had guided them in the desired direction so that connections could be made. Before they could settle into the game they would need to learn about the remaining chess pieces. The teacher pointed to the poster and talked about the king, queen, and the knight, and reminded them to look at their copy of the poster. The students worked in groups of four and, for the next 20 minutes were assigned to talk within their group about the positions of the pieces. They were instructed to move the pieces around as if they were playing the game. The teacher's role was to walk around the classroom to listen and observe.

On day four, they were ready to begin playing the game. The teacher decided to group them once again, hoping that by playing two against two, they would talk about moves and strategies with a partner. The partner-talk would enable them to think out loud as they discussed strategies and would also permit them to support one another.

Before the game playing the teacher wanted to make a few last comments about the game and the strategies for playing. The students were to think about how they'd begin, what pieces they would move first, and what their goals for the game would be. They were then told to begin their game. The teacher, as on previous days, was free to observe, listen, and guide.

The first 10 minutes of day five was spent talking about the games from day four. The teacher asked, "How did the chess game progress?" "How far into the game did you actually go?" They talked about the time involved with thinking about moves and strategies. This wasn't a game to be pulled out, played, and put away in 10 minutes time. The students discovered just what was involved in playing the game. The remainder of day five was spent the same as day four, pairs of students played other pairs of students.

The teacher decided that for days six, seven, eight, nine, and ten the students would begin to play one another, no more partners. The teacher used the information gained during observation time to match students; some students seemed to be stronger while others seemed to be having more difficulty catching on. On the sixth and seventh day, the teacher tried to match students according to their ability, but for days eight, nine, and ten, the teacher mixed the abilities hoping they could help each other. The strong ones could challenge the weaker ones, the weaker ones could learn something more about strategies and moves from the stronger ones.

The ten day units were completed and the tournament was about to begin. Students drew straws to be matched with their opponents and the elimination games began. How were the two approaches to instruction different? Is it possible to decide which class might win, based on the kind of instruction? Since this is purely hypothetical, no one can truly answer, but we hope this is something to ponder.

PROFILES

This chapter includes the profiles of 12 elementary educators. In each of the profiles, once the educator and the educator's thoughts and actions are described, a discussion follows. The discussion includes how these thoughts and actions relate to the *Curriculum and Evaluation Standards for School Mathematics* (grades K–4) (NCTM, 1989), the *Professional Standards for Teaching Mathematics* (NCTM, 1991), and the *Assessment Standards for School Mathematics* (NCTM, 1995).

Note to the reader: We focus attention on the K–4 *Curriculum and Evaluation Standards*. The NCTM authors consider the grade level categories (K–4, 5–8, and 9–12) to be arbitrary; the categories, "... are not intended to reflect school structure" (p. 6). We hope you will seek out the remaining NCTM *Curriculum and Evaluation Standards* to become better informed at all levels.

MATHEMATICS THROUGHOUT THE DAY

Mathematics can be integrated into all areas of the curriculum, as well as into many daily classroom activities. This is the philosophy of Mary Foote, a first/second grade teacher at PS 84 in New York City. She uses mathematics as students lineup to leave the room, as they ready for snack, when they read stories, when they seem to have an extra 5 minutes, and in other content areas, whenever possible.

Ms. Foote uses various attributes when lining students up or just moving from place to place. As they lineup, she'll call for those wearing blue shirts, or students wearing tennis shoes, or those with short sleeves.

Who lines up first is not as important as how she wants students to consider the attributes; she makes certain she uses visible, concrete categories. There are times when five or six students haven't lined up yet and she might ask, "What attribute can you think of that will include everyone who is left?" Ms. Foote always finds this question makes for interesting discussion.

Snack-time can be considered a problem-solving activity; she asks, "If everyone at your table gets three crackers, how many crackers will you need at your table?" She says, "Children who need more experience get called on most often." She often lays food items out on a tray in the form of a "living graph." Then she asks comparison questions, "How many more cream-filled cookies than chocolate chip cookies?" When serving fruit she may cut an apple into fourths or a pear into thirds while asking, "How many people will this apple (or pear) feed?"

Ms. Foote enjoys using literature in the classroom. She read *Ten Black Dots*, by Donald Crews. The picture book begins with a question, "What can you do with ten black dots?" and continues, "1 One dot can make a sun or a moon when day is done. 2 Two dots can make the eyes of a fox or the eyes of keys that open locks." Once she has read the book they begin a discussion of the number of dots that might be found in the entire book. They talk about other pictures that can be made with black dots, then she has them make their own book, one that is similar to *Ten Black Dots*.

Sometimes, Ms. Foote finds that she has 5 free minutes, before going to lunch or going home for the day. She fills in this time with pattern activities. She snaps her fingers, or claps her hands, or stamps her feet using an "abba" pattern. An "abba" pattern might be "clap, snap, snap, clap," or "snap, stamp, stamp, snap." The children must listen to and watch her pattern, then imitate the pattern; sometimes she asks them to the rhythm of the pattern but use a different movement or action.

She also enjoys incorporating mathematics into other content areas. The class was exploring a social studies unit on restaurants. They made clay pizzas with two and three toppings then looked at the various combinations of pizzas. As they examined and compared the pizzas, they made Venn diagrams of the different pizzas and also sorted and graphed their preferences. They were able to make many visual representations of the pizza preferences which helped them with the concept of classification.

Another segment of the restaurant unit called for naming the restaurant. They decided to take a vote on the name and wrote choices on pieces of paper. As they tallied the pieces of paper they taped the papers to the wall in the form of a bar graph. They were able to discuss and compare the results and conclude which name was most popular.

Ms. Foote says her mathematics program is very "activity based." It seems that mathematics is in some part of her mind at all times, and whenever she can link it to the topic of the moment, she makes that connection. She is much too modest when she says these activities seem, ". . . pretty routine to me."

DISCUSSION

Ms. Foote realizes the importance of connecting mathematics (*Curriculum Standard 4*) to the world outside. She makes those connections whenever possible, and she appears to be meeting the *Curriculum and Evaluation Standards'* goal of developing mathematical power for all students. By providing students with such a wide array of mathematical experiences they see how mathematics impacts all the facets of their lives.

When students lineup, they must look at themselves as they consider attributes. She wants them to be able to make distinctions as they categorize information (a step towards collecting, organizing, and describing data — *Curriculum Standard 11*).

This one activity also includes problem solving (*Curriculum Standard 1*) and reasoning (*Curriculum Standard 3*). When she asks students to decide on a final grouping that will include everyone who is left, they must consider the attributes and think of some way the attributes can fit together.

Any mathematical topic might emerge during snack-time. When children are asked how many crackers will be needed at a table if each child gets three, they are developing concepts of whole number operations (*Curriculum Standard 7*). If there are four children at a table, some will count, "One, two, three . . . four, five, six . . . seven, eight, nine . . . ten, eleven, twelve." Some may be able to count, "three, six, nine, twelve." They are adding, yes, but some are also building in the concept of repeated addition, which, they will learn later, is how they will begin multiplication.

Ms. Foote also promotes the interpretation of data (*Curriculum Standard 11*) when she creates the "living graph" with food. Students must look at the foods and count as they decide how many foods of each kind. They also make comparisons when she asks how many more of one kind than another. They also have the opportunity to add and subtract as they interpret the food graphs.

She provides them with basic lessons on fractions (*Curriculum Standard 12*) as she serves fruit. *Standard 12* states, "All work at the K–4 level should involve fractions that are useful in everyday life, that is, fractions that can be easily modeled," (p. 57). Students see how Ms. Foote cuts the apple into four slices and names it fourths and they are able to tell her what she has done.

Equally important at this stage of their learning is that these lessons are verbal. The students are not instructed to know numerator and denominator, they are not told to write one over four. The discussion moves in the direction of understanding what it means to cut an apple into fourths (four pieces) or a pear into thirds (three pieces). Once the apple or pear is cut they can see how classmates are given equal portions of the fruit.

Literature is another tool for helping students make connections to mathematics. While listening to *Ten Black Dots* the students were developing numeration and number sense (*Curriculum Standard 6*). They listened, looked at pictures, then had the opportunity to create their own books. By having students create their own books, Ms. Foote was reinforcing their understanding of number sense and numeration. She was also giving them some creative freedom to explore and express themselves in the form of art work and they were able to see a relationship between mathematics and art because of this activity.

Children have many opportunities to imitate patterns (*Curriculum Standard 13*) in Ms. Foote's classroom. Whenever she has a few extra minutes she practices patterns with the students. Instead of being a paper and pencil task, this task forces students to listen to and visualize the patterns. By listening to and imitating the patterns they come to realize the structure of the patterns that the core repeats.

Students in Ms. Foote's class see how mathematics can be meaningful in their world. When they created their restaurant and made pizzas, they were given another opportunity to classify information and interpret data (*Curriculum Standard 11*). Creating Venn diagrams was one way to organize the information — they created a visual representation of pizzas having different toppings. They could explain, by looking at the diagrams, that some people preferred pizzas with one topping while others preferred two toppings. By sorting and graphing the same information, Ms. Foote was guiding them to make connections, to see that there were many ways to organize information.

Again, they were given a graphing activity. They voted on restaurant names and, once tallied, made a bar graph that showed all choices, including the most and least favored names. Ms. Foote has shown her students quite a variety of ways to organize information and they have seen that just about any kind of information can be organized.

All of the tasks created by Ms. Foote prove to be tasks that develop mathematical thinking (*Professional Standard 1*). The students are excited and interested and always seem willing to respond. She designs the tasks around the concepts she believes to be important as well as relevant. By making the tasks relevant, they take place when students are lining up or eating snacks, they become worthwhile as well. It is important for students to know just how many crackers they will need at a given table, otherwise the amount distributed may not seem fair.

The tasks also encourage discussion. Ms. Foote facilitates discourse (*Professional Standard 2*) and encourages her students to engage in discussion (*Professional Standard 3*) as often as possible. She asks questions that prompt them to think out loud, and she makes sure that students are given equal opportunity to talk and listen.

The tools for enhancing discourse (*Professional Standard 4*) are varied. It would seem that Ms. Foote could pick up anything in the classroom and create a mathematics lesson. In just a few examples, she has shown how to use food, clothing, books, and pieces of paper (voting on restaurant names) to develop mathematical thinking as well as talking.

Listening and observing are used often as Ms. Foote assesses students' understanding (*Assessment Standard 1*). She can listen to determine if students are making connections to and drawing conclusions about ideas. By providing her students with a wide array of activities, activities that help them see the ways mathematics is used in everyday situations, she can see if they are gaining the mathematical power that has been her goal.

Ms. Foote's questions are often open-ended, allowing for many answers. When she asked students to decide a way to group the remaining students she was asking for any and all ideas. This was a time students could show what they know (*Assessment Standard 3*). Asking open-ended questions can promote equity; by offering a unique idea to the class, students can be praised for that uniqueness. This is the kind of praise that not only encourages students to continue expressing their own ideas, it is also the kind of praise that promotes self-esteem.

By taking these classroom situations out of the context of a "math lesson," Ms. Foote's children are seeing that mathematics is a part of everything they do in their day-to-day lives. We believe if we could spend 2 weeks in Ms. Foote's classroom we would find all of the *Curriculum and Evaluation Standards* integrated into instruction.

Ms. Foote says her school has multiage class groupings at first/second and third/fourth grades, but the school has straight Kindergarten and fifth grades. She teaches in one of the nine first/second grade classrooms.

CONTACT

Mary Foote
PS 84
32 W. 92nd Street
New York, NY 10025

INTEGRATING THEMATIC UNITS INTO INSTRUCTION

The Southmost Elementary School is buzzing with change. They have developed a thematic approach to teaching. Korine Garza said the thematic approach was developed ". . . to make curriculum relevant and interesting." She and the teachers of Southmost Elementary School spent one Spring identifying major themes and talking about what children would find interesting to study. As the teachers developed units, they recognized the importance of including students in the creation process, and by including the students, teachers were able to gain better information about the students' interests.

During the development stages of thematic units the teachers made certain they incorporated the Texas Essential Elements (what the state of Texas deems essential for students, at each grade level, to learn) as well as exit behaviors (what the teachers hoped students would know after instruction); they wanted to check and insure success. Ms. Garza and the teachers met many times that spring; the early meetings were mainly coplanning meetings. The project, from the beginning, according to Ms. Garza, ". . . has been a team effort." Presently, they meet for study groups; they view training tapes and dialogue about the message of the films, and they read and discuss articles. Ms. Garza feels they have been very successful, "During our 1993–1994 school year we were on probation. We got off probation because of an increase in scores — and the local (new) superintendent had an expectation that we would achieve higher scores than the state average. We increased by 15% and felt very successful. The superintendent is very student-oriented and has pushed for more teacher training in order to better work with the children."

Some teachers at Southmost Elementary School found change difficult, but Ms. Garza noted, ". . . with more training even the teachers who are more traditional . . . they are coming in more often, on Saturdays . . . they are becoming more professional." She sees much change in the school atmosphere. One of the first projects, as units were implemented, was to examine how faculty dealt with students. "They became a more focused staff and are now dealing with more issues . . . as well as the students. The students are super excited about learning. A consultant came in and modeled coopera-tive learning. The students want to learn that way all the time. The students are so excited about the thematic units."

Southmost Elementary School spends a great deal of money to improve their thematic units. During the 1994–1995 school year, they spent $10,000 on manipulatives and will spend the same amount in the 1995–1996 year. Staff development is a major component to the thematic units. Consultants come to the school to work with the teachers — sometimes during the week and sometimes on Satur-days. When the consultants are scheduled to visit, Ms. Garza brings in substitute teachers to replace the teachers who wish to attend the meetings.

One of the school's initial concerns was the improvement of mathematics test scores. The school's philosophy was to have more of a hands-on approach to mathematics. Ms. Garza said the admini-strators began, "... to analyze how we teach math — textbook driven with few manipulatives. There was not much challenge to students and we wanted to try to get teachers away from it, so we began to work for the hands-on approach."

The teachers maintain communication throughout the year because of the thematic units. These units are schoolwide; when pre-K begins a unit, all children through fifth grade begin similar units. They began the 1994–1995 school year with "All about me and family." This unit lasted 6 to 8 weeks. This unit has subtopics such as "our bodies changing and growing" and "family life." One of the activities in "our bodies changing and growing" looks at student growth from infancy to the present. Students study, then plot and graph their growth. This is a good time to make comparisons and discuss those comparisons.

"Family life" encompasses many areas of family. One of the local grocery stores is a sponsor at Southmost Elementary School and they send many circulars of grocery items, including specials of the week. The students and teachers talk about family budgets; the students are given a budget then have to buy groceries with their money. Sometimes, they don't have enough money, then they have to look for better buys — they have to do some comparison shopping.

"Family life" also has students take a look at their own families. They build family trees and trace as far back as anyone in their family can remember. They look at their family unit and graph the number of brothers and sisters. Once again, they can compare results and decide who has more, who has less.

Ms. Garza believes this is a good way to begin the year because it is an enjoyable way for everyone to get to know each other. The children learn more about their cultures and they can develop a good sense of themselves.

DISCUSSION

"All about me and family" connects students with their own families and cultures. This unit helps them make connections (*Curriculum Standard 4*) from one mathematical topic to another, as well as see connections between mathematics and what is real to them — their families. Children spend a great deal of time talking about budgets and comparing their shopping ideas; they talk about how they've grown and compare their past height to present height or their present height to someone else's height. The communication (*Curriculum Standard 2*) in the classroom is stronger because of the units; they are given many opportunities to think out loud as they make those comparisons. Mathematics becomes real to them, they see a purpose to what they are learning.

In "All about me and family," the children learn statistics (*Curriculum Standard 11*). They learn different ways to collect and interpret data as they chart and graph information. They interpret information as they balance budgets, as well as when they try to measure and compare their height or weight. Measurement (*Curriculum Standard 10*) also ties in to the height and weight activity. When students measure their heights, not only do they practice skills of measuring, they also experience a real-life application for using rulers.

When students are given a family budget to comply with, they have to break down that budget. To decide what they will spend when buying groceries, they must be able to estimate (*Curriculum Standard 5*), then compute (*Curriculum Standard 8*). Once they have estimated the cost of groceries, they do the actual figuring of cost. The opportunities for whole number operations, as well as interpreting data, are endless when dealing with budgets.

Ms. Garza and the faculty at Southmost Elementary School have put in immeasurable hours designing this curriculum. By including students in the decision-making process, the faculty has shown how they value their students. Together, they have developed worthwhile mathematical tasks (*Professional Standard 1*) for the classrooms. These tasks have created enthusiastic students. The students are also experiencing great success; they are happy in the environment that their teachers have come to value.

The students spend more time in problem-solving and cooperative learning situations. This is promoting discourse in the classroom (*Professional Standards 2, 3, and 4*). To compare their heights or the size of their family, teachers must provide questions, children must use some tool for measuring, and must then discuss their findings. The creation of thematic units has the whole school talking and integrating the units into instruction has been uplifting for the everyone involved.

Much of the work that the students do is observable. When they chart information, the teacher is there to observe and assess (*Assessment Standard 1*). The teacher can ask, "Are they able to apply their mathematical understanding to these situations?" When they talk about their family size, the teacher can listen as they compare. By listening and observing the teachers are able to check for understanding.

The units are geared to meet the individual needs and interests of the students. The students share what they know about their families and feel good about the contributions they make to the classroom. By assessing students based on what they can share, teachers are able to promote equity in their assessment (*Assessment Standard 3*).

The thematic approach is really working for the teachers and students at Southmost Elementary School. It has been a 4-year process to get the thematic units into place, but it has been a worthwhile, successful project. Ms. Garza and the teachers at Southmost Elementary School continue to meet and plan as they build on the units, making them stronger and even more appealing.

CONTACT

Korine Garza
Instructional Facilitator of Curriculum
Southmost Elementary School
5245 Southmost Road
Brownsville, TX 78521

LIFE SITUATIONAL MATHEMATICS: DESIGNING A NEW PLAYGROUND

Tackan Elementary promotes a variety of schoolwide mathematics projects. Most recently, they have emphasized life situational mathematics. Instead of using a textbook that creates a problem, the school tried using something that made sense to children — a problem the children needed to solve. The latest project was the students' reorganization of the playground. Dianne Wetjen of Tackan Elementary says, "Adults were listening to the frustrations of kids in overcrowded spaces. Children learned the real math problems of running a school with limited monies."

Ms. Wetjen said her school was "... having some problems on the playground during recess." When the administrators looked into what was happening, they found that poorly defined and perceived space zones were contributing to the children's frustrations — the students felt overcrowded.

Students representing each classroom met with the student council. Ms. Wetjen reported that because of the discussions during student council meetings, "We began to look at the ways we perceived the playground. Children perceived the space differently because they spent the most time out there ... playing. They noticed the position in which the aides were placed and thought of a better way to position the aides so they could see more areas of the playground." The student council representatives came back to their classrooms to discuss the meetings. Much time was spent problem-solving. As students considered ways to recreate the playground, they had to think about what kinds of games they would play and if any of those games would require special space. Then they had to decide how much space was needed to play the different games. They took measurements and decided on a tag area and the girls wanted a special, small area for themselves. As they tried to redefine the playground, they found mathematics to be a useful tool to help solve their problems. They persuaded the P.T.A. to help buy soccer balls for the playground, too.

Ms. Wetjen believes that challenging children with real-life problems helps children appreciate the natural connections between mathematics and everyday, relevant situations. "When given the chance to think abstractly, the children were attentive, full of ideas, and took the whole matter very seriously," remarked Ms. Wetjen. The students worked to solve a problem that held some meaning for them and the teachers. The teachers and administrators found that children were working cooperatively with each other as well as with adults (another facet of real-life problem-solving).

Discussion

The project of recreating the playground encompasses many of the *Curriculum and Evaluation Standards*. The project in itself was a project in problem-solving (*Curriculum Standard 1*); this was part of the students real world, so it was a real-life problem to them. Being a real-life problem with students working to find solutions, the need for mathematical connections (*Curriculum Standard 4*) was equally as real. They no longer saw mathematics as a set of isolated topics; they estimated, took measurements, dealt with mathematical computation, and collected data.

To solve their real-life problem, they had to collect data (*Curriculum Standard 11*) by observing children at play to see what kind of games they were playing. They continued that collection of data when talking to other children to find out what games were important to them. Once it was decided what games and activities children wanted to play on the playground, they estimated (*Curriculum Standard 5*) playing space and made measurements (*Curriculum Standard 10*). Space was being visualized, remembered, compared, and explained. Children were constantly counting and estimating distance, the people involved, balls needed, games being played, etc. They even estimated the time needed to walk to the playground from the cafeteria.

As they took measurements, their number sense (*Curriculum Standard 6*) continually developed. They could see relationships between number and measurement, as well as between number and whole number operations (*Curriculum Standard 8*). Their measurements didn't always come out evenly, therefore some discussion and attention focused on fractions, decimals, and rounding. This was a first-hand look at how these concepts were used in everyday life. The students also spent time focusing on whole number operations, as well as fractions and decimals (*Curriculum Standard 12*), when they had to consider how they would spend the limited amount of money in the budget.

When looking at the playground, they had to consider the space carefully, then take into account geometric concepts (*Curriculum Standard 9*) about space and angles as they drew their plans for the playground. Communication (*Curriculum Standard 2; Professional Standards 2, 3, and 4*) had to be ongoing if they were to be successful in the project: where would the soccer nets be placed; where did the girls want their special space; how much space would each activity require?

This was a worthwhile mathematical task (*Professional Standard 1*) that no teacher had to introduce. This task came directly from the students out of a problem they were experiencing in the school. Students felt comfortable discussing the problems and talking to other students about possible solutions.

We believe that this sort of discussion would not have been possible if the teachers and administrators had not created a secure learning environment for the students (*Professional Standard 5*). Their continuous discussions as well as work times for measurement and calculations were more proof of the teachers having developed the environment and provided students opportunity for classroom discourse.

The major analysis of students' work comes from the completed project. The students can now more happily and safely spend time on the playground — the playground that they recreated. They have experienced success at a deeper level, deeper than scoring 100% on a mathematics test. The teachers were able to assess students' learning as they looked at the successful completion of the project (*Assessment Standard 2*) — "... the observation of students' work can reveal qualities of thinking not tapped by written or oral activities" (p. 13).

As the students created the playground project, individual interests emerged. Each student had an opportunity to demonstrate his/her strength during the project (*Assessment Standard 3*). The teacher took this time to assess students' abilities to collect information, take measurements, and make estimations, as well as calculations. By incorporating life-situational mathematics into instruction, teachers and students alike found an avenue to work constructively, have a good time, and create a strong, successful learning environment.

Dianne Wetjen has recently retired, but at the time of the author's first conversation with her she was an NCTM speaker and a teacher at Tackan Elementary School, 99 Midwood Avenue, Nesconset, New York 11767.

CONTACT

Dianne Wetjen
1690 Rainbow Court
Marco Island, FL 33937

HELPING STUDENTS MAKE MEANING: A PROBLEM-SOLVING APPROACH

Beverly Boggs, a second-grade teacher at Circleville School, has gone through quite a change since becoming involved in Project H.O.M.E (Hands-On Mathematics Education). The trainers in the project, led by the National Diffusion Network, worked with teachers to foster strategies to strengthen mathematical literacy for elementary students. As participants (one of which was Beverly) met each summer for 3 years, they were given opportunities to use manipulative materials, learn more about problem-solving and questioning with students, and incorporate writing strategies into their mathematics curriculum.

Ms. Boggs, one of three teachers chosen from her county, spent the first summer session (1 week) learning about manipulatives. "So when we trained other teachers we knew exactly what we were doing." A concern of Ms. Boggs's was how would she ". . . be able to get it all in?" Her first thoughts were that incorporating manipulatives into instruction would be overly time consuming. But, she ". . . made a commitment to try it all — I knew I was going to have to go back and train other teachers so I gave it my all." After her first summer at the institute, and 1 full year of implementation in her own classroom, she knew she would be better equipped to teach teachers. She could bring with her some credibility — it had worked for her.

Ms. Boggs was most excited about her students reaction to her discoveries. She said they really began to like mathematics. Although no longer involved in the project, the 3-year project having been completed, Ms. Boggs continues using the methods learned in her classroom.

Ms. Boggs began the 1994–1995 school year by bringing a watermelon to class. The first classroom task was to estimate how many seeds were in the watermelon. Of course, the only way to find out for certain was to eat the watermelon. They saved the seeds and, once dried, the students began to count them. This was one way Ms. Boggs got them to learn about grouping while counting. Students began counting and Ms. Boggs would get them confused by talking while they counted. They would get (slightly) frustrated and say they had to start over. She got them to realize they should group by tens then count; this was how she introduced counting and grouping.

Then Ms. Boggs posed some problems. She usually wrote problems that dealt with the students' environment. Evan counted 16 seeds. His friend David had 18 seeds which he gave to Evan. How many seeds did Evan have? Ms. Boggs provided students with base ten blocks and let them discover there were just too many units when they counted out 16 and 18. Since they already had counting, grouping, and regrouping practice, they didn't have any trouble regrouping the ones for tens with their base ten blocks. She was able to provide them with successful experiences because of her own Project H.O.M.E. experience.

Project H:O.M.E. spanned three summers, 1 week each summer. The first summer, training was geared towards improving student success with understanding mathematics with manipulative use. The teachers became the students. They worked with manipulatives much the way they would have their students work the following year. The teachers were provided with manipulatives to use for 1 year. The next summer, the training began with a refresher of the last session. Then, the teachers were trained to train other teachers. One of the project's requirements was that the participants conduct a workshop with teachers in other counties. The third summer, discussion revolved around the NCTM *Curriculum and Evaluation Standards*. The participants presented their work on a curriculum strand to area administrators—they demonstrated how the *Standards* could be found in the mathematics curriculum beginning with Kindergarten and moving through the higher grades.

Although Ms. Boggs was the only one who attended from Circleville School, the project still had an effect on the entire school. As the school was in the middle of textbook adoption, Ms. Boggs and the other newly trained teachers were able to recognize necessary components of a textbook that would facilitate effective instruction. They chose a textbook that incorporated the standards into instruction, and also one that provided educational materials. They were able to procure additional materials with Eisenhower funds.

When Ms. Boggs begins teaching a new concept, she always begins with manipulatives, providing students much opportunity to examine the manipulatives and their properties. She still considers practice to be an important part of instruction, but waits until she is certain that her students have a firm foundation from which to work.

When asked, "What do you want for your students?," Ms. Boggs said, "I want them to be able to understand mathematics, to understand what we are doing, and to really know why that answer is the way it is." Ms. Boggs knew she had gained a lot from the project. While relaying this story she began to reflect, "Last year, we went on a field trip. On the back of the seats on the bus, the students noticed odd and even numbers on the seats. They recognized a pattern on the seats." Her students realized mathematics was not just found in the classroom, and after getting off the bus they continued looking for other patterns.

DISCUSSION

Ms. Boggs jumped right in on the first day of school promoting problem-solving (*Curriculum Standard 1*) and estimation (*Curriculum Standard 5*). The watermelon sparked the students' interest. Estimating the number of seeds is not only a fun activity for the students, but it also gives Ms. Boggs a chance to find out what they know about number and quantity (*Curriculum Standard 6*). She lets them problem solve as they count the number of seeds — she doesn't tell them that there is a "best" way to count or group, she wants them to realize that grouping by tens would be more efficient. This practice is also setting them up for additional work with grouping, place value, and making exchanges.

Students can relate to the word problems Ms. Boggs writes. The problems deal with the environment that surrounds the students. They live in a rural area, so many of the problems revolve around farmers, the countryside, and animals. She strives to help them make connections (*Curriculum Standard 4*). When she noticed students making connections on their own, for example, noticing the even and odd number patterns in the school bus, she felt truly successful.

Ms. Boggs has created an environment built on her knowledge of the *Curriculum and Evaluation Standards*. In this case, her commitment to Project H.O.M.E. is apparent when listening to her discuss her actions in the classroom. Her teaching embodies the *Professional Standards*. She asks questions that deal with her students' environment. The students can see that she thinks about them and incorporates their environment into instruction (*Professional Standard 1*); she poses tasks that are based on "knowledge of students' understandings, interests, and experiences" (p. 25).

Ms. Boggs provides her students with a variety of tasks that promote a positive feel in the classroom (*Professional Standard 5*). She stands back and lets the students explore and express their thoughts. Ms. Boggs has created a comfortable, secure environment, providing an arena for students to learn mathematics in an enjoyable manner. Not only does she use the materials supplied by the textbook company, she also brings in outside resources — the watermelon!

When a teacher gives students an opportunity to problem solve, independently or in groups, then that teacher has the freedom to listen and observe (*Assessment Standard 1*). Ms. Boggs was able to learn about students' beliefs about number sense as they estimated the number of watermelon seeds. She was able to see what they were thinking as they grouped the seeds. Her work was validated when students noticed patterns outside of the mathematics classroom; their knowledge was more than sets of unrelated facts and pieces of information — they had arrived (*Assessment Standard 5*). She gained information about their learning from a variety of sources, not just the paper and pencil test at the end of the week.

Ms. Boggs was happy to be a participant in this project. Now, she is confident and can use manipulatives more effectively. She is happy that her school now has what other counties have — a variety of manipulatives. She and her fellow teachers also have a new understanding of strategies for teaching mathematics.

CONTACT

Beverly Boggs
Circleville School
PO Box 9
Circleville, WV 26804

COMPUTERS AND MATHEMATICS:
ANOTHER APPROACH TO PROBLEM-SOLVING

Kristine Diener, with the help of "a creative elementary staff," has been writing quite a range of computer programs. Ms. Diener and her staff believe they are a resource for elementary teachers in their district. Teachers often call the district office to say they are addressing beginning multiplication or that they have done everything they know how to do in subtraction and that they, and the students, need more help. If they don't already have something written that will address the needs of the teacher and his/her students, Ms. Diener and her staff create new programs.

For many years the schools in Ms. Diener's district had computers, but the computers were slow, taking up to 45 minutes to load a program. The teachers mainly used the computers for drill and practice. Ms. Diener spent a couple of years lobbying to replace those computers. When the computers were replaced, she wanted to make certain the teachers were comfortable. Since the computers had been slow and the old programs were mainly drill and practice, Ms. Diener said, "There was some damage to undo." Many of the teachers held on to the bad feelings about the old, slow computers. A great deal of effort went into training the children and the teachers. The trainers stayed in the schools the first few weeks the computers were in place to make certain everyone was feeling comfortable with the computers.

Since it was felt that the teachers had previously identified mathematics time with computer time, Ms. Diener chose not to put any mathematics programs on the computers that first year. Instead, she chose to install "Kid Pix" (an alphabet program that showed each letter of the alphabet, voiced the letter, then stamped it down on the screen). Children were able to study the letters and their sounds at their own pace; some matched sounds to letters very quickly, while others needed much longer. The computer activities gave them the time and space needed.

Kid Pix was a comfortable and fun way to move into mathematics. The teachers felt they could use a language approach to mathematics, leave out the drill and practice, and use a variety of simulations. The skills that they practiced fell more under the notion of classifying and categorizing than under practicing the basic facts of mathematics.

Ms. Diener said they have developed over 300 pages for grades Kindergarten through 6. They have used Kid Pix to do a literature-based reading program and have then made connections between mathematics and the reading that they are doing. Kid Pix provides problem pages that relate back to reading.

For example, the children are given a problem called "17 Kings and 42 Elephants." They take a trip through the jungle looking for 17 kings and 42 elephants. Along the way they encounter many animals and birds, and must keep track of the number of animals and birds they see. They tally their information and then make a graph. They can either make a graph on paper with pencil or right on the computer, and they have a choice of making a picture graph or a bar graph. "Kid Pix" provides the students with a tool box, a way to describe the data.

As they tally their information and design their graphs, students work cooperatively with a partner. They have particular roles and must realize the responsibility of that role. Some discussion time may be necessary because, as Ms. Diener states, they may have different ways of tallying and graphing the information. Some children may see parrots, monkeys, and apes, while others may see animals with four legs, animals that stand on two legs, and animals that fly.

When the students have completed their graph they can print it out. Not only can the teacher see how the students were thinking, but the students can also compare to each other. They can observe the various ways that information can be collected and classified.

Ms. Diener has been working on this project for 6 years. "We are asking teachers to be risk-takers. We are not asking them to be the expert anymore. Along with this paradigm shift we must provide them with support." She justified her statement and the need for continued support because, as she stated as our conversation came to a close, "The way most of us learned is the way most of us teach."

DISCUSSION

Promoting problem-solving (*Curriculum Standard 1*) is at the core of the Kid Pix program. When children sit down to read "17

Kings and 42 Elephants" they encounter a problem situation. They work with a partner and discuss with that partner the best way to collect and organize information. As they problem solve they are also communicating (*Curriculum Standard 2*) with one another. They may have different ideas of how to organize and tally the information; they see another's perspectives and must decide which direction to take. The decision-making process takes additional communication between the two children.

"17 Kings and 42 Elephants" also immerses children in *Curriculum Standard 11, Statistics and Probability*. They read a problem, collect and organize information, then design a graph. They must have some prior knowledge of the various kinds of graphs, because it is their choice whether to make a bar graph or a picture graph.

Another choice is whether to draw the graph or use the computer to make the graph. Assigning two children to work at a computer is bound to generate some noise. The problem-solving process linked to the computer provides a powerful tool for enhancing discourse (*Professional Standard 4*).

The students are attracted to the graphics of Kid Pix and are very eager to work on problems provided. The problems provided, in turn, have been created in a way that will promote mathematical thinking. The problems, as stated earlier, also promote discussion (*Professional Standard 3*). This discussion time is also a reflective time; students listen to each other and try to decide which approach to take. They explore alternatives.

When the teacher observes students exploring alternatives, assessment can be made based on students' thinking (*Assessment Standard 1*). In what ways are the students thinking about solving the problem? How are they collecting data? How are they classifying and organizing the information? What kind of graph did they choose to make? Did they choose paper and pencil or the computer to make their graph?

Teachers also gain a very tangible form of assessment from the students. Students display and discuss their graphs when finished (*Assessment Standard 2*). The teacher sees, firsthand, the information students have chosen to include. The teacher can see how information was categorized and classified, how information was interpreted and placed on the graphs, and if the students have an understanding of graph design — do they know how to construct a bar or picture graph?

"17 Kings and 42 Elephants" is just one example from the Kid Pix program. The program includes a wide variety of problems as well as stories that will comfortably integrate literature and mathematics.

CONTACT

Kristine Diener
Waukesha School District Office
222 Maple Avenue
Waukesha, WI 53186

TEACHING ALGORITHMS: A VARIETY OF APPROACHES USING TECHNOLOGY

When the National Council of Teachers of Mathematics (NCTM) came out with the *Curriculum and Evaluation Standards* (1989), Mike Rooney was pleased to see that the NCTM took the same approach he did. He said, "We need to be giving kids lots of alternatives. Learning styles are so varied in schools, it is the instructors job to give kids more than a single basal approach to mathematics." Mr. Rooney wants to provide those various approaches for teaching mathematics.

Mr. Rooney said his real outlet is reaching other teachers. He is "Mr. Goodmath" — he wears a lab coat covered with numbers and he broadcasts the "Mr. Goodmath" show from the media center at his school, Welleby Elementary. The only thing teachers must do is turn on the televisions in their classrooms. Mr. Rooney presents a variety of approaches to working a variety of mathematical problems. His programs often consist of his explaining the concept/topic of the lesson. He writes a problem then talks about it as he solves it. This demonstration is followed by two children who work, then talk about how they solved similar problems.

In his television shows, "Mr. Goodmath" presents alternative ways to add, subtract, multiply, and divide. In one video, he explains a way to add numbers using a method called plus/minus addition. He presents a problem, 29 + 68, in horizontal form. He promotes working problems mentally and says, ". . . ask your students to pick whichever addend they want, and add up to a 10. Let's take, for example, 29. To add 29 up to a 10, what we need to do is add one — giving us a 30. This makes it much easier to add." "Mr. Goodmath" feels 29 + 68 may be too difficult to add mentally, but 30 + 68 would be easy, getting 98 for an answer. He continues, "What we need to do is to remember that we changed the addend by 1, by adding 29 up to 30, but now as far as this sum (98) is concerned, we need to subtract 1 giving us the difference of 97. This 97 is the sum of 29 + 68."

This example is just one of many. "Mr. Goodmath" demonstrates a way to add columns of multidigit numbers. He emphasizes, as he talks, that by using this approach, Hutchings Low Stress Addition, "students never have to add more than basic addition facts." This approach is a systematic, organized way to handle numbers by adding two digits at a time and recording work on the paper. As students record they not only record the ones but also tens. "Mr. Goodmath" believes that once children have developed an understanding of adding numbers, then these techniques, like calculators, can free the children from lengthy computation so that more time can be spent problem-solving.

He also challenges a grade level to a problem of the week. Students respond to him by writing their solutions in a letter format. The fifth grade students at Welleby Elementary sort mail for Mr. Rooney. They go through the mail, screen letters, and look for clever solutions. Then, on television, "Mr. Goodmath" looks at the clever solutions and features those children on the following week's show.

Teachers react positively to "Mr. Goodmath." He conducts in-service workshops throughout the state and many requests have been made for the videos he has produced. Mr. Rooney developed a 22-minute awareness program. He stated, "If teachers wanted to start the program at the school level they could, all they need to do is see this tape." His teaching methods have been noticed. In 1991, Mike Rooney was one of three teachers in the country recognized by the National Science Foundation Presidential Awardee Program for Teaching Math and Science (his award was specifically for math). He was also recognized in *Learning* (1992) and given a Professional Best Award. He knows that teachers have taken bits and pieces of "Mr. Goodmath" and have tailored the program to fit their needs. Mr. Rooney has talked to some district supervisors who ". . . are reporting frequently that teachers are making direct applications in their rooms and that 'Mr. Goodmath' is making an impact in the schools."

"Mr. Goodmath" is a registered trademark and Mike Rooney is a busy man. He teaches fifth grade at Welleby Elementary, produces his "Mr. Goodmath" show, is adjunct faculty at Florida Atlantic University, and is writing his doctoral thesis. He has also been developing video-telecommunications from his classroom — students can actually communicate with him while they are watching. Unfortunately, this project is on hold because of a loss in funding, but Mr. Rooney continues to look for other funding sources.

DISCUSSION

Mike Rooney stresses communication (*Curriculum Standard 2*) during his lessons. During his videotaped instruction, he models his work then he asks students to solve similar problems and explain their actions as they work. They are spending time not only listening but also explaining; this is one way to reinforce the concepts they are learning.

Mr. Rooney believes that students need to be shown a variety of ways to solve problems. This is one reason why he provides students with examples of the plus/minus addition and the Hutchings Low Stress Addition. He feels that students don't always understand one way of solving a problem and one of these other methods may just make it "click" for them. He is helping them see the relationships (*Curriculum Standard 4*) between the mathematical ideas of whole number operations (*Curriculum Standard 8*).

"Mr. Goodmath" presents a strong example for providing tools for enhancing discourse (*Professional Standard 4*). In this example, he is providing the students with new ways to think about mathematics — a most valuable tool! He gets students to talk about their thought processes and wants to ensure that they will all be able to solve problems; therefore, he gives them the tools that will be necessary.

By providing them with tools, "Mr. Goodmath" is trying to help them develop mathematical power. He wants them to be successful and to be able to make connections from one example of the operation to another. He is also promoting equity (*Assessment Standard 3*) among students. He knows that one student might understand one method, while another may understand better if given a different method for solving the problem. He would never say, "There is only one way to solve this problem."

Mr. Rooney has developed a program that has far reaching implications. Teachers from all over the state of Florida are tuning in to watch and the children are his biggest fans.

CONTACT

Mike Rooney ("Mr. Goodmath")
Welleby Elementary School
3230 Nob Hill Road
Sunrise, FL 33351

MATHEMATICS, MUSIC, AND MNEMONICS

Marilyn Anderson believes that children learn best through a variety of experiences and she has provided her Kindergarten students with many situations/experiences for learning. When she feels confident that they understand the concept, she adds an amusing twist to their learning.

The twist was born as she worked on her first degree — music. She teaches her students rhythmical activities (many rhyming words, lots of clapping and snapping fingers) that she has composed. The activities reinforce the concepts students have learned. She says the activities can also be considered mnemonic devices, ". . . after you've done the thinking there is still some amount of memorization. If we have given them many experiences with concrete ideas, they still need some way of remembering." Ms. Anderson believes that children remember much more easily when they have rhythmical experiences.

Ms. Anderson wants children to ". . . enjoy math, to have fun with it and gain an understanding of problem solving, number sense . . . to understand as much as they are capable of and have lots of experiences with manipulatives, so when they are ready to move on to more advanced problem solving they will have had plenty of experiences." Her previous bouts with frustration when teaching third grade, pushed her to develop and introduce the rhythmical activities. She believed her students understood what they were doing but just couldn't remember their facts quickly enough.

Ms. Anderson's rhyming activities are in alignment with the topics taught. While children are learning basic facts, they are often introduced to the concept of learning to add doubles $(1 + 1, 2 + 2)$. She taught them to say the following rhyme:

Double your learning, double your fun,
Learn your math fact doubles, one by one.
$1 + 1, 1 + 1, 1 + 1$ is 2 (snap)
$2 + 2, 2 + 2, 2 + 2$ is 4 (snap)
$3 + 3, 3 + 3, 3 + 3$ is 6 (snap)
$4 + 4, 4 + 4, 4 + 4$ is 8 (snap)

etc., to $9 + 9$. As the students repeat this rhyme, they have fun and at the same time they memorize those facts.

The intention of a rhyming activity that was written mainly for her third grade students to help with remembering fraction equivalents. The "Pizza Chant" is one that she and her students repeated often:

> Pizza, pizza, it's so good
> Let's talk about pizza so, fractions can be understood.
> One whole pizza, cut in equal pieces
> Two halves, four fourths, or eight eighths
> If you eat two fourths, or four eighths
> One half is, what you ate.
> One half, two fourths, or four eighths
> This is all the same on your plate.
> Fractions can have many different names
> Equivalent fractions are all the same.
> If you eat two halves, four fourths, or eight eighths,
> You would eat the whole thing.

Ms. Anderson often uses a keyboard in the classroom. She says anyone can use the keyboard, ". . . playing a tune isn't necessary, just push one of the rhythm buttons. The students can repeat the rhyme to a rhythm such as rock or rap."

The children learn and enjoy spending time in Ms. Anderson's class. Her present activities, now that she teaches Kindergarten, are tied closely to counting and calendar activities. The class spends time looking at different groupings of numbers, then Ms. Anderson presents her "Fiddle Faddle Counting" exercise. The students alternate between clapping their hands and patting their hands on their legs. For example, when they say "fiddle" they pat (indicated by "y"). When they say "faddle" they clap their hands (indicated by "x").

> Fiddle faddle, liddle laddle,
>   Y   X   Y   X
> Dinosaurs in shoes.
>   Y   X Y X
> Riddle raddle, diddle daddle,
>   Y   X   Y   X

I can count by 2's.
Y   X   Y   X
2,   4,   6,   8,   etc.
Y X Y X Y X Y X Y X

Continue, using the following rhymes:

Dinosaurs with fleas, 3's
Indoors, 4's
Alive, 5's
Do tricks, 6's
In heaven, 7's
On a date, 8's
Be mine, 9's

Ms. Anderson creates and uses these rhyming activities with her own students, but often shares them with other teachers. She does training sessions in her school and district and presents at some national conferences.

DISCUSSION

Ms. Anderson is giving students the opportunity to make connections (*Curriculum Standard 4*): "... the study of mathematics should include opportunities to make connections so that students can link conceptual and procedural knowledge" (NCTM, 1989, p. 32). The students in Ms. Anderson's classroom spend a great deal of time developing concepts and ideas. Ms. Anderson makes certain that they work and manipulate objects, and that they have time to discuss ideas. The rhyming activities are a time for making connections to help them memorize facts and basic information that will help them in subsequent lessons.

When she introduces the skip counting rhyme, she is reinforcing their number sense (*Curriculum Standard 6*). They may already have some sense of skip counting, by twos, threes, and sevens, but seeing the numbers as they say the rhyme and hearing other students count strengthens their sense of number concepts. As they say their rhymes together, they are hearing number patterns emerge (*Curriculum Standard 13*). This is often a point of discussion in Ms. Anderson's classroom, and seeing the number patterns is an additional means for strengthening their sense of number concepts.

Although singing or clapping out rhyming activities might not seem like a task, we believe it falls under planning worthwhile mathematical tasks (*Professional Standard 1*). Ms. Anderson has developed what she believes are worthwhile tasks in that they display a worthwhile product. Students enjoy the activities and can see that Ms. Anderson wants them to learn and have fun in the process. The learning environment has developed nicely in this classroom — the students are eager for the chance to sing or clap out the rhyming activities they know, as well as learn new ones (*Professional Standard 5*).

The activities developed by Ms. Anderson enhance students' mathematics learning. Her earlier reasoning for developing these activities was to build on their understanding and help them retain basic concepts (*Assessment Standard 2*). That reasoning was based on her assessment of how her students were understanding concepts. She continues to assess as she listens and observes during rhyming activities — one way to make inferences about what her students understand.

Ms. Anderson's goal is for students to have an understanding of a concept before the rhyming activities begin. While they are engaged in the rhyming activities, she asks herself, "Are they joining in or are they following behind?" If they are following behind, they may not be at a strong level of understanding or perhaps they haven't memorized the rhyme. She will check with a child individually, if that is the case, to examine his/her understanding.

The creativity (and time) involved in developing the rhyming activities says a great deal about Ms. Anderson as a teacher. She wants her students to enjoy learning and she wants her students to be successful in her classroom. No doubt there is laughter to be heard coming from Ms. Anderson's classroom.

CONTACT

Marilyn Anderson
T.C. Cherry Elementary School
1001 Liberty Avenue
Bowling Green, KY 42104

GAME PLAYING DURING MATHEMATICS INSTRUCTION

Encouraging mathematical thinking through games is Mary Behr Altieri's approach to teaching. Ms. Altieri is a Chapter One teacher, teaching children in grades 2 through 6. She has spent 13 years as a Chapter One teacher and 12 years as a regular education teacher. Instead of pulling students out for instruction, she works with the teachers and students in their classrooms. She introduces and reinforces mathematical concepts with a variety of games.

Her motivation to use games comes from some early experiences. During her first year of teaching second grade, she did a pilot study for the Open Court Publishing Company (LaSalle, IL). She found that there were many games embedded within their programs. This experience made her look for more ideas and games, as well as ways to adapt games originally designed for older children for use with her second graders. Also, early in her teaching experience, she found that all teachers, in all grades at her school, played Quizmo every Friday afternoon (similar to Bingo but instead uses basic mathematical facts). Some students appeared to be having fun, but Ms. Altieri realized it was a game that produced the same winners each week. There were many who never won; only the children who knew the right answers and had the basic facts well-memorized were rewarded. This experience compelled her to find games that would provide challenges and promote mathematical thinking.

Ms. Altieri looks at the textbooks as she considers topics, then draws from the many games she has collected. She has been collecting games throughout her teaching career. She said, "If we teach the map instead of the directions they will know how to get from here to there."

Ms. Altieri believes that teachers may be in the habit of asking children questions they already know the answers to and, in that sense, children don't have to think. If children can't figure out answers fairly quickly, then they don't want to bother. In a game situation, children are given questions they have to think about, and Ms. Altieri finds they are always willing to pursue the game.

When Ms. Altieri and one of the authors spoke, they played an addition "roll a problem" game. Ms. Altieri said it was a good practice game that would involve some thought and would incorporate place value and probability. The game began with each player making a 2 x 2 grid (the spaces eventually hold two 2-digit numbers taking on the form of an addition algorithm). Then, Ms. Altieri rolled a number cube, numbered 0 through 5, and each wrote the number rolled into one of the four spaces; altogether she rolled the cube four times. The object of the game was to place the numbers in such a way as to make the largest sum. The one who made the largest sum would be the winner.

Since Ms. Altieri now teaches all elementary grades, not just second grade, she can use this game in many ways to work with many levels. Older children can play "High-Low" in which she uses two cubes, one numbered 0 through 5 and the other 5 through 10. The children make a 3 x 3 grid. She rolls the high cube twice and the low cube twice. Again, they try to make an addition problem with result being the highest sum. Of course, Ms. Altieri might change the rules (at any moment) and have students make the smallest sum. She likes to think of these games as a form of "mental gymnastics."

Ms. Altieri has many games that can be incorporated into most any mathematical topic. She has become quite a resource for the teachers in her school. Working with many new, young teachers has made for ongoing staff development. She believes that new teachers feel isolated, ". . . they are given a set of textbooks and a class list." She says her door is always open and she is very willing to work with any teacher. While Ms. Altieri doesn't have units developed or the games described in book form, she believes it will be a future project.

DISCUSSION

When Ms. Altieri plays dice games with her students, she touches on a few of the *Curriculum and Evaluation Standards*. She provides games that force her students to look at mathematics as problem-solving (*Curriculum Standard 1*) — they are trying to decide which numbers would best fit in which column in order to gain the highest score. As they try to decide, they are also reasoning (*Curriculum Standard 3*). She is getting them to make connections between these whole numbers, the whole number computation involved in the addition algorithm, and how the positioning of the numbers affects possible outcomes — in this case, the sum (*Curriculum Standards 4, 6,* and *8*).

Since they are deliberating about possible outcomes, they are also beginning to think about probability (*Curriculum Standard 11*) — "If I place this 5 in this column, what are the chances of rolling another 5?" When Ms. Altieri wants to move into other lessons that include probability, this lesson may be the foundation for students' connections.

Ms. Altieri also adheres to the *Professional Standards*. Incorporating games into instruction confirms that she spends time thinking about what her students would enjoy, what might call their attention to learning new topics. The students have a good time and they certainly think the games/tasks are worthwhile (*Professional Standard 1*). Using the games is also a wonderful way of providing tools for enhancing discourse (*Professional Standard 4*). The students are given time to talk about their reasons for positioning the numbers, ones column or tens column. The "roll a problem" game becomes a springboard for thought and discussion. Ms. Altieri used the materials to lead the way to develop the discourse in her classroom.

For Ms. Altieri to be successful with games and discussion of ideas, she had to pay careful attention to the environment (*Professional Standard 5*). She wanted her students to talk, to think out loud. She gave them the freedom to exchange ideas in a comfortable, secure environment. She established autonomy in her classroom.

Whether introducing topics, or supplementing or extending mathematical topics through game playing, Ms. Altieri assesses her students' understanding by listening and observing (*Assessment Standard 1*). She promotes games that encourage their mathematical power. Ms. Altieri keeps written records of students' learning. She prints students' names on mailing labels (one name per label). She walks around the classroom with a clipboard (the labels are attached to the clipboard) and writes comments directly on the labels. She has that immediate visual, when looking down at the labels, of who is successful and who might need addition help. She keeps a record of each student and adheres the labels directly into the student's file.

Ms. Altieri listens and observes, then uses the outcome of the activities as a basis for discussion (*Assessment Standard 2*). She might ask, "What if you could look at the algorithm you just made and move the numbers around?" Students' responses are very telling.

Their answers say a great deal about what the students know about number and place value.

By providing a variety of games, Ms. Altieri is insuring that all students will find an aspect of mathematics that will empower them and that all students will be successful. She is promoting equity (*Assessment Standard 3*). She also gets a good picture of her own teaching as she checks their understanding.

The "roll a problem" game is just one of the many games Ms. Altieri uses with her students. In this one example, her actions have included the first four *Curriculum and Evaluation Standards,* as well as whole number computation and probability. She has also connected with the *Professional Standards* and the *Assessment Standards.*

CONTACT

Mary Behr Altieri
Van Cortlandtville Elementary School
Main Street
Mohegan Lake, NY 10547

LITERATURE AND MATHEMATICS

Lois Moseley took two of her interests, literature and mathematics, and combined them to form culturally relevant activities. When asked how this idea came about, Ms. Moseley said, "In the Houston area, there are so many different cultures. Students often don't see themselves as special or know a great amount about their own culture. There are books and activities that, when taken to the schools, can help children make connections to all cultures." Her ideas began to develop when she was a mathematics teacher in Houston Independent School District (ISD). She noticed that some children could do any mathematical problem that was provided, but their success was due to their skill of solving a problem, not any understanding of the content of the situation. Her goals were for children to gain an understanding of mathematics as well as feel good about themselves.

Ms. Moseley wanted to find areas of students' strengths and build on that. She felt the best way to do that was through literature; through an integrated curriculum. She often uses a story as a springboard for children to find out more about a culture. As they study the culture, they begin to find out about inventions from that culture, farming techniques, architecture, and the culture's use of mathematics. Much time can be spent on mathematics as it can be tied into the inventions, the farming, and the architecture.

Ms. Moseley's position as a consultant for Region IV Education Service Center in Houston, takes her into many schools. She supervises projects in schools and partnerships with business schools that are undergoing change. She also spends time in low-performing schools, the schools in which Region IV promotes the use of alternative strategies. When looking at TAAS (Texas Assessment of Academic Skills) scores, Ms. Moseley says the African Americans have scored lowest on all portions of the test and, as a result, most of the projects in the low performing schools are campuses that have high African American or Hispanic populations — another reason she feels making cultural connections is so important. It is in these schools that she has permission to ". . . try radical things."

There are four schools that Ms. Moseley works closely with, visiting them on a regular basis. She spends time with teachers, watches them teach, shares strategies, and gives them lessons to try. The teachers are videotaped, or they videotape themselves. Later they evaluate their own performance and, as Ms. Moseley says, "Can see and reflect just what they do from the students' point of view." She says she still does a great deal of teacher training and takes every opportunity to provide them with literature for the classroom.

Ms. Moseley provides teachers with the literature through a packet entitled, "Hands-On, Literature-Based, Culturally Relevant Mathematics Activities." Once a story is told, problems are posed; for example, teachers can read, *The Indian in the Cupboard*, by Lynn Reid Banks, or just tell children the story of Omri. The following story and activity is included in Ms. Moseley's packet:

> This is the story of Omri who receives a three-inch high plastic Indian for a birthday present. He also received a cupboard from his brother and the old key to the cupboard from his mother. Before going to bed, Omri places the plastic Indian in the cupboard. In the morning, the tiny Indian, Little Bear, has come to life.
>
> Some Indian tribes, including those that lived on the Plains of the United States and in the Woodland areas of Canada, ate mainly meat. The Pueblo and other farming groups lived chiefly on beans, corn, and squash. Corn was an important part of the diet for many Native Americans. Originally corn was much smaller and was shaped somewhat like a pine cone. Each of the kernels was completely enclosed in a tough, pointed husk. The Native Americans used ingenuity and selective planting to produce better crops of corn.
>
> Native Americans did not grind their entire corn crop. The ripe ears were eaten as a vegetable, being boiled with the husk on. They also ate the tassels which are rich in protein. Popcorn was also cultivated and it was used both for eating and decoration. Husks were used to make floor mats and woven decorative items.

Once the story is told, discussion and activities may begin. For example:

- ◆ Some people eat popcorn with nothing on it. Some like butter on their popcorn. Some like butter and salt. What do you like to put on your popcorn?
- ◆ Cut out a 2 x 2 inch square piece of paper. Draw popcorn with your favorite topping on it. Use a bulletin board to make a bar graph, and place your drawing in the proper category. What is the most popular topping in your class?

Children not only make a connection to the Native American culture, but can also connect to something most of them like — popcorn.

DISCUSSION

This story can be the impetus for children to begin to make comparisons such as who likes what kind of popcorn? No matter the age, they are reasoning (*Curriculum Standard 3*) as they make those comparisons. They are also involved in statistical operations (*Curriculum Standard 11*). They are provided with graphing experiences — each student posts his/her favorite topping, then they all look at the graph. As they interpret the graph, they are communicating (*Curriculum Standard 2*). They talk about what they see — what is the most popular topping and what is the least favorite topping? The children cut-out paper, make a bar graph, make comparisons, discuss their findings, and in the process have read or have heard a piece of literature, a piece of history.

The children are able to make connections, linking mathematical topics to their own cultures. This has a double bonus of not only letting children see how mathematics is a part of their culture, but also giving them an opportunity to learn something about their own history.

The nature of these lessons will be of interest to the students. They will be eager to learn about their culture. Using Ms. Moseley's ideas will prove to be worthwhile for the students and the teachers (*Professional Standard 1*). The students may find a new sense of self-worth and the teachers will find truly motivated students.

When students make comparisons of favorite and least favorite popcorn, they are drawing some inferences about what their peers like to eat. This is connected to *Assessment Standard 1* that draws on the mathematical power students should possess. The teacher can assess a student's mathematical power as the student makes connections, comparisons, and draws inferences. The teacher can also learn a great deal by listening to students as they discuss the graphs and make their comparisons.

Since Ms. Moseley asks teachers to reflect on their videotaped lessons, they have an opportunity to assess themselves. They learn about their own teaching styles and their students' learning styles. At the same time, students learn about their cultures and find out about the contributions their cultures have made to modern civilization. This is a time they can share some bit of their own uniqueness (*Assessment Standard 3*); when they can connect with some aspect of their own culture. A student may find that one place within him/herself that will shine above all the other students.

CONTACT

> Lois Gordon Moseley
> Coordinator for the Department of General Education
> Region IV Education Service Center
> 7145 West Tidwell
> Houston, TX 77092

MAKING CONNECTIONS BETWEEN
MATHEMATICS AND SCIENCE

The Indianapolis Zoological Society has a strong commitment to educating the children of Indianapolis and, for more than 6 years, Deb Buehler was a facilitator of many of the exciting programs at the Indianapolis Zoo. She shared the Zoo's goals, one of them being to write curriculum with an interdisciplinary approach which would help students realize the ways mathematics was used at the Zoo. One aspect of her job was to think about what students might do while visiting the Zoo. She planned workshops for teachers and provided kits that teachers checked out for use in their classrooms. Another goal was to promote awareness, interest, understanding, and an appreciation of animals and plants.

Ms. Buehler worked collaboratively with the Indianapolis Newspapers, Inc., Newspaper in Education Office, and the Indianapolis-Marion County Public Library. Together they developed articles for "Read the Zoo," which continues to provide exciting articles for children and which are printed using larger type so children will find it easier to read. The articles appear once a week for 9 weeks; the students receive fact cards and posters, and they get the newspaper in their classroom each week.

One issue of "Read the Zoo" included an article about the African Pygmy Goat. It was an informative article, describing the goat, how it looks, what it eats, and how it lives. The article also addressed some of the reasons people raise goats. Comprehension questions followed the story. Also included was a list of books (the goat being the subject) that could be found at the local library.

"Science for Conservation" is a Zoo sponsored program for fourth and twelfth grade students. This program promotes science careers and highlights lifelong learning. Students explore the mathematics and language skills conservation biologists need to be successful. Ms. Buehler wrote curriculum that detailed the work of diverse conservation biologists. The curriculum was written to be both interdisciplinary and to reflect skills/tools that scientists use in their efforts to protect wildlife. She creates problems such as: How big is the population in the wild? and How do scientists make estimations? Ms. Buehler invites scientists to visit. "Science for Conservation" begins with the guest scientist participating in a teleconference, visiting a local classroom, and presenting an evening lecture. It is a full day for the scientists, but Ms. Buehler never has difficulty finding guest scientists for the program. Word gets around in the science community and scientists are eager to participate. To them it is a great honor to be part of the program.

"Science for Conservation" extends into the schools. Participating schools receive the *Indianapolis Star* or *Indianapolis News* with an article describing each scientist, a poster of the scientist, and the curriculum developed by Ms. Buehler. The curriculum includes a background information section, a description of the scientist, activities and extension activities, and a reading resource list.

One example of the curriculum details marine biology. It begins with an article, "Natural History — Sea Turtles," and is followed by a discussion with the conservation biologist, Roderic Mast. There are three activities with objectives: Map Reading and the Sea Turtle — students will be able to plot sea turtle nesting sites on a world map; Sea Life Survival — students will be able to explain the factors affecting wild sea turtle survival; and Population Estimation — students will be able to estimate a population size. These activities integrate language arts, science, and mathematics.

The Indianapolis Zoo also collaborated with local elementary teachers and Indiana University faculty to put together the "Zoo Connection," a series of topics and activities geared for two levels: Kindergarten through third grade and fourth through sixth grade. The "Zoo Connection," funded by a grant from the Indiana Commission on Higher Education, provides integrated curriculum resources for teachers and students particular to the Waters Biome at the Indianapolis Zoo. "Zoo Connection" includes students' activities for the Zoo visit as well as activities to be completed in the classroom. Ms. Buehler facilitated the writing efforts of the teachers by helping them gain an understanding of Zoo operations. By collaborating with teachers, the Indianapolis Zoo is better able to respond to student and teacher needs.

An example taken from "Zoo Connection" for Kindergarten through third grade is entitled, "Cetacean Station." The students observe whales or dolphins at the Zoo then identify habitat and general characteristics of whales and dolphins. The skills students use for this activity include observing, communicating, measuring, classifying, and comparing. The lesson begins in the classroom with the students estimating the length of a whale or a dolphin. Once they have discussed and compared their estimations they will compare them to the actual size when they get to the zoo. It is a rich activity that once again integrates content areas.

Ms. Buehler also managed student workshops at the Zoo, hiring contractual instructors to teach the workshops. She taught via technology through distance learning. She collaborated with another teacher to put together five units for instruction. These units, which included mathematics proficiencies, were written to fit into the science curriculum. She truly created activities that integrated language arts, science, art, and mathematics.

DISCUSSION

"Read the Zoo" and "Zoo Connection" are filled with ideas and activities that, as a whole, meet many of the *Curriculum and Evaluation Standards*. By integrating the newspaper into instruction, Ms. Buehler is helping to promote good readers while showing students that the newspaper is filled with wonderful information that can be relative to their lives. Once children have read from the newspaper, they begin to talk about the articles. They are being given the opportunity, by the teacher, to communicate (*Curriculum Standard 2*), to exchange ideas and information.

Whether they are reading the newspaper, one of the stories included in the curriculum, or one of the books from the booklists, they are reading and making connections (*Curriculum Standard 4*). By integrating literature and mathematics, the students are finding out some of the ways mathematics is used in everyday life, not just in the mathematics classroom.

When the students learn about marine biology, they get to learn about map reading. This, in turn, leads to learning statistics and geometry (*Curriculum Standards 9 and 11*). It is an opportunity for them to gain information about handling data and about plotting a graph. They also learn about the map and the world, as they study turtle nesting sites.

Measurement and estimation are often found in the curriculum (*Curriculum Standards 5 and 10*). The students estimate population sizes when they study marine biology. In another lesson, they must estimate the length of a dolphin, then when they go to the Zoo they can learn more about their estimations and predictions. They get to see, first hand, how their estimates match the real thing.

This curriculum is filled with worthwhile mathematical tasks (*Professional Standard 1*). Ms. Buehler has been continually delighted with the students who come through the Zoo with smiles on their faces. They call out, with enthusiasm, as they make connections between what they have been reading at school and what they are seeing at the Zoo.

The materials that the Indianapolis Zoo provides offer many opportunities for teacher and student discussion (*Professional Standards 2, 3, and 4*). Students also have a chance to talk to the guest scientist who answers any questions the students may have. The curriculum seems to be created around opportunities for students to wonder, to question, and to look for answers.

The teachers can assess how students are thinking as they observe the students questioning, responding, and working (*Assessment Standard 2*). The activities include objectives and contain work for students. Once they read maps, they must look for nesting sites and be able to plot those sites on the map. Once students have heard a story about out sea turtles and talked to the conservation biologist they must be able to talk or write about the factors that affect sea turtle survival. Teachers can look at the objectives and check the students' understanding. Ms. Buehler has created programs that integrate good assessment practices as well as many content areas.

CONTACTS

Deb Buehler
Education Manager
San Antonio Zoo
3903 N. St. Mary's Street
San Antonio, TX 78212

Deborah Messenger
Manager of School Programs
Indianapolis Zoo
1200 W. Washington Street
Indianapolis, IN 46222

PROMOTING MATHEMATICAL THINKING THROUGH DISCOURSE

Asking questions is one way to promote discourse in Priscilla Smith's first grade classroom. She wants children to explain their thinking and tries to ask questions that will do just that. Some of the questions she asks are:

Does anyone have a different answer?
Can anyone do it a different way?
Does anyone see a pattern?

One of Ms. Smith's goals, when listening to students, is to elicit children's solution methods. She bases her teaching on students' questions and responses. She makes many decisions throughout her day. Those decisions are dependent upon the students' knowledge — she may have to provide them with more information, back up to an earlier topic, or jump ahead and help them make connections to new information.

The three questions Ms. Smith asks can be fit into a framework developed by Judith Fraivillig of Northwestern University. The framework, Advancing Children's Thinking (ACT), was developed while observing and interviewing Ms. Smith as she worked to promote children's mathematical thinking during instruction. As Ms. Smith focused on students' explanations, Dr. Fraivillig could see three overlapping components emerge. She labeled the components Eliciting, Supporting, and Extending (Fraivillig, 1995). According to Dr. Fraivillig, by eliciting children's solution methods the teacher can ". . . orchestrate learning opportunities for all students while assessing individual children's thinking." By asking if anyone can work a problem differently or if anyone sees a pattern, Ms. Smith not only promotes discussion in the classroom, but also gains the opportunity to hear how her students think.

Ms. Smith also supports her students' mathematical thinking. Ms. Smith uses positive reinforcement as well as humor as she supports their thinking. She listens then helps them make connections, providing bridges which help them to link one idea to another. If a student has difficulty solving a problem, she may only need to remind him/her of a similar problem that was solved earlier or she may need to repeat or rephrase what the student is trying to verbalize.

The third component, extending children's mathematical thinking, can be found in the ways Ms. Smith poses challenging tasks and promotes classroom discussions. She sets high goals for her students and pushes them to accomplish these goals. She encourages students to analyze and to compare. When they provide her with one answer she pushes to get them thinking about alternative answers. One day, after class had ended, a student volunteered a comment about the order of addends (interesting that students in Ms. Smith's class continue to ponder mathematical concepts after class). The student said that the order in which addends are written does not affect the sum. Ms. Smith posed, "Is that true for addition and subtraction?" Ms. Smith acknowledged the student's puzzlement and then forced the student to continue thinking about the original question as well as study the relationship between addition and subtraction.

On another occasion, she asks them to look at the tiles on the floor and decide how many squares they see. Ms. Smith said, "If a child says 10, that is fine; if one says 15, I tell him to show us. That lets the other kids see how you can get more." She is modeling ways of extending their thinking — asking them questions, getting them to show what they know.

It is not always easy to isolate the three components of ACT. There are times when the components overlap. While Ms. Smith might elicit the thinking of one student, she may be extending the thinking of another; her support may be ongoing. She provides more information than they may be ready for, but Ms. Smith feels sure some may want to hear it and the others will connect with it later.

Ms. Smith hasn't always been open to accepting a variety of responses in her students. The change began about 10 years ago when she attended a workshop. She found ". . . another way of looking at things." Slowly she began to change her teaching style, then 4 years ago some Northwestern University faculty came to her school to work with teachers. "I was thrilled — many were not thrilled. Two I worked with hated it. . . . One of most vocal now really loves it."

Ms. Smith's teaching revolves around the questions that she asks. Her students do most of the talking, now. They can learn new perspectives from each other, and Ms. Smith can learn more about her students' thinking.

DISCUSSION

Ms. Smith's questions promote problem solving in the classroom (*Curriculum Standard 1*). Her questioning compels students to think differently, to look for alternative solutions. Therefore, just as the *Curriculum and Evaluation Standards* promotes, problem-solving does permeate the mathematics curriculum in Ms. Smith's classroom.

Standard 2, Mathematics as Communication, also plays a major role in Ms. Smith's classroom. Children are learning the language of mathematics as they talk and as they listen. She asks students to explain and justify their thinking which promotes critical thinking.

Ms. Smith encourages students to look for patterns (*Curriculum Standard 13*). This is a general question she asks in many lessons, not just those set aside for looking for patterns. Looking for patterns in all lessons helps students see relationships and make connections to other mathematical areas and beyond . . . where they see patterns will always hold a new surprise.

Ms. Smith knows her role and the students' role in discourse (*Professional Standards 2* and *3*). She sees the value in giving students time to talk. She has learned a great deal by listening to her students and knows they are learning from each other.

She created a secure environment for her students (*Professional Standard 5*). She let them know the first of the school year that laughing at a peer when he/she talks or asks a question would not be permitted. This rule has made it easy for students to ask questions whenever they don't understand, and if they do have a problem she makes certain she helps them as soon as possible. These actions tell the students that their ideas are important — that they are important. She also pushes them to tell parents and visitors what is going on in the classroom. When parents stop by her classroom, the students are eager to show what they just learned. The parents are impressed; the students get a review and build their self-esteem at the same time. Since the visitors and parents are so impressed, the students feel a new sense of success and self-esteem — another way Ms. Smith shows support for her students.

The three questions Ms. Smith asks allow for continuing assessment. She gets immediate answers but at the same time tries to extend their thinking. In this way, she promotes their mathematical thinking (*Assessment Standard 1 and 2*) — they answer questions yet continue to learn as she pushes for more information.

The students are comfortable with differing answers. Ms. Smith acknowledges all answers, letting the students know that their answers are important, that she values their individuality and independence (*Assessment Standard 3*). The varying answers give her clues as to where each child is in his/her thinking.

The questions that Ms. Smith asks and her perspective towards children's thinking can guide any mathematics lesson. They key is to learn to ask then listen. Sometimes it is difficult to wait for students to answer. A concern for many teachers is time constraints — having to finish a lesson or a chapter in a certain amount of time. If students are given more opportunity to talk, they will learn much more from their verbal reflections than they could ever learn if teachers just told them what to do. Priscilla Smith, presently teaches third grade, but believes her actions and questions hold true for any grade.

CONTACT

Priscilla Smith
Kingsley School
2300 Green Bay Road
Evanston, IL 60201

USING GEOMETRY TO ENCOURAGE ARTISTIC EXPRESSION

Attending a 1994 state mathematics conference was just the beginning for Jean LaGrone. She attended a workshop in which two teachers shared units they had done in their own classrooms. Both teachers described how they studied geometry using artwork and architecture.

When Ms. LaGrone left the conference she began searching for sources of traditional art from other cultures. As she looked for books, she set the following criteria: (1) It was necessary that stories accurately portray life in a particular culture or tell a traditional tale; (2) The books needed to include illustrations portraying traditional art or designs from the culture; and (3) The illustrations needed to detail clear examples of geometry concepts. She found many books in the multicultural section of the bookstore and she now connects the literature to multicultural education, social studies, writing, science, and geometry with the result being student-produced artwork. Each week she teaches a geometry concept to her second graders and uses the concept in an art project that relates to the study of a culture. These artwork samples are studied and admired, then used for the purpose of assessment.

Ms. LaGrone has a sequence she follows as she introduces a geometry concept. She begins by reading a book to the class. They look for the location of the culture on a map then talk about the climate and lifestyles of the people. They study the illustrations in the book and look for clues that may lead to a discussion of cultural similarities and differences in clothing or customs, in family and community. After the discussion, Ms. LaGrone rereads the book; this time they look for geometric patterns in the illustrations. She keeps the lesson focused on the geometric concept because she plans for students' to connect their observations to the art project that will follow. The art project, derived from the culture addressed in the text, is the assessment piece for each geometry lesson.

For example, Ms. LaGrone began a lesson by reading *Welcome Back Sun* by Michael Emberly. *Welcome Back Sun* describes a traditional Norwegian holiday in which families celebrate the return of the sun after a long, dark arctic winter. Once she had read the story, she began a discussion with her students. She stressed the importance of family relationships as well as the celebration. They looked for Norway on the map and talked about what the climate might be like. She asked students to compare the book to a book they had read the previous week, *Huan Ching and the Golden Fish* by Michael Reeser. She used a Venn diagram to record students' comments about how the two stories were alike and different.

Ms. LaGrone reread the book and asked students to examine the patterns on the sweaters worn by the characters in *Welcome Back Sun*. The goal of the lesson was to help the students identify the pattern as a tessellation. They looked back at the illustration of a fish kite in *Huan Ching and the Golden Fish*; she wanted them to notice the tessellation in that illustration as well as the tessellation in the sweater. The scale on the kite fish used a closed curve as the repeating pattern and the sweater used a polygon. They compared the two shapes and talked about the different curves as Ms. LaGrone guided them to observe the scale as being a closed curve. She gave each student a cutout of a single shape from the kite scale tessellation and a blank sweater pattern. She then asked the students to use the cutout to design a new sweater for the father to wear as he welcomes back the sun.

Ms. LaGrone was able to assess the success of this lesson ". . . by the student's ability to use specific geometry skills and discuss the cultural application of geometry in the art project." She found that her students were beginning to identify geometry in traditional cultural designs from around the world. She said that they also became more skillful at creating art using geometry and began to use compasses and rulers to create repeating patterns during free time. They explored the patterns they made and noticed the "different sized corners" in the shapes which set the scene for a lesson about angles. The children began to notice patterns all around them, one student came to school and said she saw some "really cool wallpaper with polygons and a tessellation."

Ms. LaGrone believes that "regular exposure to literature based on different cultures has increased students' awareness of cultural diversity around the world." In the classroom, when someone asked, "What is culture?," she defined it as "the different ways people show respect or have affection or other emotions for each other. Culture is apparent in the way we dress, live, and behave." She wants students to realize that common feelings and attitudes can be expressed in a variety of ways. In closing she stated, "Geometry, taught in this format, is far more than a few basic shapes. It is a vibrant part of our daily world."

DISCUSSION

The mathematics curriculum should include the study of geometric concepts (*Curriculum Standard 8*), ". . . so that students can recognize and appreciate geometry in their world," (NCTM, 1989, p. 48). Ms. LaGrone teaches one geometric concept each week and based on what the students say (about seeing patterns on buildings or in wallpaper), they truly recognize and appreciate geometry in their world.

Students are learning about cultures and are making connections (*Curriculum Standard 4*) between the cultures and geometric concepts. As they study clothing they find patterns in the designs. In *Welcome Back Sun* and *Huan Ching and the Golden Fish*, they found that by drawing the patterns (*Curriculum Standard 13*) in a particular way, tessellations are formed. Within the patterns they detected polygons as well as closed curves then had a chance to draw the shapes which helped to extend their understanding of the shapes.

These activities do extend the students' understanding of concepts which means the tasks they are asked to complete facilitate the development of their mathematical thinking (*Professional Standard 1*). Ms. LaGrone asks them to create new patterns based on the patterns observed and discussed. The creation of new patterns reflects their mathematical thinking.

Listening to children describe their patterns, as well as examining the final product (the artwork), enables Ms. LaGrone to analyze students' understanding of the concepts (*Assessment Standard 2*). While students describe their patterns, they continue to make sense of the activity. This sense-making portion of the lesson, students talking and listening to each other (*Professional Standard 3*), enhances mathematics learning.

Ms. LaGrone says, "I encourage them to talk to each other while doing math and listen to their talk to assess their understandings. I keep regular anecdotal records of their use of math concepts and skills, and use these records to shape new experiences." Since her district has complete inclusion and she frequently teaches mixed grade levels she believes it is, ". . . extremely important to choose activities that can be presented in a way to meet the different developmental needs of all my students." Ms. LaGrone provides tasks that allow for these different needs (*Assessment Standard 3*). The students bring different experiences to the class and are given room to express themselves in their final product (their artwork).

Ms. LaGrone was selected as the 1996 Nebraska Teacher of the Year. She was also selected to be one of the featured teachers on a series called Teacher to Teacher with Mr. Wizard. Teacher to Teacher is funded by the National Science Foundation in conjunction with Nickelodeon Network and the Mr. Wizard Foundation. She has created the beginnings of quite a bibliography:

Culture	Title	Author
Africa, Akan	Spider and the Sky God	Chocolate, D.
Africa, Ghana	The Fortune-Tellers	Alexander, L.
Africa, West	Why Mosquitoes Buzz in People's Ears	Aardema, V.
Africa, Zulu	Shaka, King of the Zulus	Stanley, D.
Amish	Just Plain Fancy	Polacco, P.
Australia	This Place in Lonely	Cobb, V.
Aztecs	The Flame of Peace	Lattimore, D.
China	Huan Ching and the Golden Fish	Reeser, M.
China	Tikki Tikki Tembo	Mosel, A.
Egypt	Tutankhamen's Gift	Sabuda, R.
Japan	Little Inchkin	French, F.
Japan	This Place is Crowded	Cobb, V.
Native American		
Algonquin	The Rough-Face Girl	Martin, R.
Northwest	Raven	McDermott, G.
Inuit	Northern Lights, The Soccer Trails	Kusugak, M.
Navajo	The Goat in the Rug	Parker, N.
Ojibway	Dreamcatcher	Osofsky, A.
Plains	The Girl Who Loved Wild Horses	Goble, P.
Pueblo	Arrow to the Sun	McDermott, G.
Several	Ten Little Rabbits	Grossman, V.
Ute	Coyote Steals the Blanket	Stevens, J.
Norway	Welcome Back Sun	Emberly, M.
Pennsylvania Dutch	The Folks in the Valley	Aylesworth, J.

Scandinavian	Goldilocks and the Three Bears	Brett, J.
South America	The Hummingbird King	Palacios, A.
Ukraine	Nina's Treasures	Czernecki, S.
United States	Sam Johnson and the Blue Ribbon Quilt	Ernst, L.

CONTACT

Jean LaGrone
Westgate Elementary School
7802 Hascall
Omaha, NE 68124

3

PUTTING IT ALL TOGETHER: A REAL-LIFE PROBLEM IS SOLVED

The following profile provides an excellent illustration of what first grade students can do when given the opportunity. Some teachers fall into a traditional role — they teach basic facts in a set order and believe that students must learn basic facts before any problem-solving can begin. It has been found that students will learn basic facts when provided with a variety of problem-solving experiences (Peterson, Fennema, Carpenter, & Loef, 1989).

As the first grade students in Marcia Hibbits' classroom solve their real-life problem, they encounter a wide range of mathematical topics. Mrs. Hibbits knows it is her job to make certain they encounter these topics — a job she enjoys very much. She continues to marvel at what her students can do when given problems to solve.

It all began when Marcia Hibbits' husband surprised her with a large, white teddy bear. She took the bear to her first grade classroom. Since the mascot of their elementary school, John Foster Dulles Elementary, was a bear, the students decided to name the bear Johnny Dulles, J.D. for short.

The children loved J.D. but found that they often had to move that big bear in order to find a place to work in their own classroom. As Mrs. Hibbitts continually moved the bear from place to place, she began to think about ways to solve the location/relocation problem. She decided that J.D. needed a house.

Before she mentioned the idea to her students, she spent a great deal of time thinking about how the class could approach the location/relocation dilemma, and decided the class could build a house for J.D. She realized the project would be an enriching, rewarding experience for her first graders. Mrs. Hibbitts' said her goals became to:

- challenge myself,
- challenge the students to apply problem-solving strategies to a situation that evolved within the classroom environment,
- use problem-solving strategies, measurement, estimation, and geometry in a single project,
- involve students in numerous hands-on activities,
- achieve many of the objectives in the Oak Hills School District course of study for mathematics in a unique way,
- explore as many mathematical concepts as possible,
- integrate mathematics, language arts, health, and science,
- achieve a useful, child-centered product for the classroom,
- experience working together to achieve consensus,
- work in cooperative groups,
- involve parents and members of the community, and
- maintain a safety-conscious environment.

She wanted to integrate content areas, address as many mathematical concepts as possible, cooperatively group students, and successfully complete the project. The preparation time and legwork were astounding. Mrs. Hibbitts sketched designs, considered a variety of materials, spoke with a friend about design and construction concerns, estimated costs of building the house, and anticipated classroom management issues that could arise. After making these considerations and inquiries, Mrs. Hibbitts was ready for students to think about and discuss J.D.'s needs.

Mrs. Hibbitts had just taken J.D. out of the reading bathtub. She asked her students if they thought J.D. needed a place of his own. Of course everyone said, "Yes!" That afternoon they began a discussion of the dilemma. The objective of the activity was for students to realize the need for a house and identify information they would need to achieve the goal of building a house. She opened the discussion by inviting the students to talk about J.D.'s needs. Although she made sketches of the house and had obtained information about building the house, she wanted the students to brainstorm a list of questions about a house for J.D. Some of their questions were: "How tall will it be? Where will it stand? What will it look like? What will it be made of? How many windows will it have? Can we build it in the room? Who will build it? How can we pay for it?" This first meeting was a time for wondering and questioning. Mrs. Hibbitts closed the lesson without answering their questions; she wanted a place to begin the next day's discussion.

Mrs. Hibbitts thought about the students' questions as she planned for the next meeting. She believed her job was to narrow the focus of the discussion and set some objectives for the meeting. She wanted them to:

+ establish a location for the house,
+ analyze possible specifications,
+ work in cooperative groups,
+ write/draw for a variety of purposes including labels,
+ measure length using nonstandard units,
+ role-play or use manipulatives to find a solution to a problem, and
+ make tables to sort information.

(The last four were district objectives.) The meeting began with the question of location. The students looked around the room trying to find the best place for J.D. and his house. They looked at each suggested site, debated the pros and cons of the site, and then made a decision based on their research. Then, using masking tape, they outlined the house to help visualize the space.

The students were able to use the floor and wall tiles as units of measurement and worked within their cooperative groups to draw the design, label the parts, and estimate dimensions. Each group was given the opportunity to measure the site and work on its design. During this one activity time, the students' actions met all of Mrs. Hibbitts' objectives.

The third activity Mrs. Hibbitts developed revolved around the final decision of the specifications of J.D.'s house. Her objectives were:

+ determine the specifications of the house,
+ achieve consensus on the specifications,
+ measure lengths with inches, and

♦   model a problem situation using numbers and/or letters.

(The last two were district objectives.) This activity began with a comparison of the students' drawings from activity two. As they compared and discussed their drawings they came to a consensus on the size and appearance of J.D.'s house. Mrs. Hibbits wondered about whether to use the floor tiles or wall tiles when considering the final measurements. One student showed concern about the type of measurement to be used, "Shouldn't the measurement be in inches?" After discussion of this question, the class decided that inches would be a more productive unit of measurement for building. As a group, they used measuring tapes on the masking tape outline in order to express the dimension in inches. Mrs. Hibbitts then chose a group of four students to draw the final sketch.

Mrs. Hibbitts entitled activity four, "Answering the Questions." Her goals for this activity were:

♦   maintain a safety conscious environment,
♦   involve a member of the community, and
♦   use the writing process as a tool for learning and thinking across the curriculum (a district objective).

Mrs. Hibbits reviewed the students original questions and found that many of those questions had been answered during the first few activities. She wanted to address the remaining questions. As J.D.'s house was becoming a reality, the students wondered about noise, safety, and the amount of space needed for daily activities.

As the students considered space and safety, they realized the house could not be built in the classroom. Mrs. Hibbitts said she had a friend who offered to help build the house but before he could help he would need to know exactly what they wanted. They decided to write him a letter and together they drafted a letter which included the house's specifications. Mrs. Hibbitts told them they would be given a certain amount of money to spend. She was referring to her room allotment money for the school year; the students said they should use it to buy materials. She agreed to that suggestion and offered to provide additional funds for the project, if necessary.

The next activity revolved around choosing the colors for the house. Once again, Mrs. Hibbitts set objectives:

- ◆ express a choice in writing,
- ◆ create a graph to report the results,
- ◆ explore meanings of a graph by making identification, comparisons, and predictions (a district objective), and
- ◆ involve students in hands-on activities.

Mrs. Hibbitts distributed small rectangular pieces of paper so that each student could record his/her color choice. The students glued the rectangles to a piece of construction paper in a way that formed a simple bar graph. They were then able to compare the results and determine that the majority of students wanted a white house with a red roof.

Their work was far from complete, though. Mrs. Hibbitts wanted the students to decide, in the next activity, how much paint they would need to paint the house. Her objectives for the activity were:

- ◆ experience converting inches to feet,
- ◆ explore the calculation of area,
- ◆ use estimates to determine amount needed,
- ◆ use calculators to work with large numbers,
- ◆ explore capacity using quarts,
- ◆ explore situations by manipulating shapes, measuring and counting, and
- ◆ explore situations for which an estimate is appropriate

(The last three were district objectives.) Mrs. Hibbitts made full-scale models (using butcher paper) of the walls so they could visualize how much paint would be necessary. They made 1-foot squares of construction paper and as they made the squares they used the fact that 1 foot equals 12 inches. With their square feet in hand, they covered the model of the front of the house. They could easily count that the area of the front of the house was 25 square feet.

Determining the area of the sides of the house was more of a challenge, since the side walls were shaped like trapezoids (in this case the trapezoids had two right angles). They covered most of the side walls, the trapezoids, then encountered a triangular shape they couldn't figure out how to cover. The class debated ways to cover the triangles. One possibility was to cut apart some of the square feet so they could cover the area more accurately. Another suggestion was to move the models in order to look at the situation differently. Then, a student noticed that if he first flipped one of the trapezoids and put the two trapezoids together they could make one large rectangle. They were able to determine that the two sides were 52 square feet. The children used their calculators to determine that 77 square feet of paint would be needed.

It was time to make some estimates. Mrs. Hibbitts had an old quart can of paint that she used as a benchmark for their estimates. By reading the can they found that 1 quart of paint would cover 80 to 100 square feet — thus, 1 quart of paint would be enough for one coat of paint on the house. Mrs. Hibbitts decided to buy a gallon can of paint, in case the house needed a second coat. She brought the gallon can of paint to the class. When they read that a gallon would cover 400 to 500 square feet, they used their calculators, and repeated addition, to discover that 1 gallon of paint could cover the house more than three times!

The problem-solving stage was completed and all the children felt they were successful problem-solvers! As Mrs. Hibbitts reflected on this project she said, "They took a deceptively simple classroom issue and solved it in a most convincing fashion. Step by step we worked our way through to success. When we share the project with visitors, every student almost bursts from the joy of understanding what mathematics has empowered us to achieve. They are eager to share all the ways in which we used mathematics to accomplish the goal." Mrs. Hibbitts believes that because of this project her students have come to value to discipline of mathematics.

Throughout this project, Mrs. Hibbitts was conscientious of her recordkeeping. During each activity she took time to observe learning as it occurred. She was careful to listen and record student comments, questions, and answers for her own records. She also kept records of each student's understanding of selected activities. Each student had a book (with four pages). One page included a record of the measurements of the completed house. The remaining pages included reflections of the processes used to solve the problems of converting inches to feet, choosing paint color, and determining paint quantity.

Mrs. Hibbitts is in her 25th year of teaching first grade. She seems to greet each year as enthusiastically as the year before. She is an active teacher. She represents the county by presenting at local and national workshops and conferences — and always comes back to teaching.

DISCUSSION

We must begin this section by saying that Mrs. Hibbitts is one organized person. Before Mrs. Hibbitts began any discussion of the project with her students, she made sure she had all the information. By being organized and prepared before the project began, she and the students would be able to jump right in. This project, a student-driven project, connects with all the *Curriculum and Evaluation Standards*.

The project was a problem-solving (*Curriculum Standard 1*) project from the beginning— from deciding where to put the house, to what it would look like, to what color it would be, to how much paint they would need. The children were intensely involved throughout the project, whether measuring, comparing, or discussing measurements and comparisons. The communication (*Curriculum Standard 2*) was strong in Mrs. Hibbitts classroom; they learned a great deal from each other as they talked. One student reasoned (*Curriculum Standard 3*) then offered the need for measuring in inches instead of the nonstandard measure of floor and wall tiles. Another student found that if they flipped one of the trapezoids they could make one large rectangle. These students were making some wonderful mathematical connections (*Curriculum Standard 4*). When students are given room to explore and then talk about their ideas, teachers may find they have underestimated their students' abilities to reason. In this case, the powers of reasoning, communication, and making connections were strong!

The initial discussion of building a house for J.D. and the meeting to decide upon a location were times filled with questions. They estimated (*Curriculum Standard 5*) the dimensions of the house and then how much space they would need for the house. The students took measurements (*Curriculum Standard 10*) of the proposed house to make certain the house would fit in the chosen location, and they also had to estimate how much paint they would need. They saw and experienced the importance of measurement.

Geometry (*Curriculum Standard 9*) was an important aspect of this project. The initial nonstandard unit of measurement was square floor tiles; they fit together many squares to make the measurements. The paper model of the house presented another geometry lesson. They used the cut-out squares to measure the house. Measuring the rectangles on the front and back were not problem, but they had to problem-solve to decide how to measure the sides — trapezoids. They were finding patterns (*Curriculum Standard 13*), when filling the rectangles with squares and they were seeing relationships between shapes when flipping the trapezoids to make a large rectangle. Since they had filled the front of the house (a rectangle) with squares, they knew that the sides would be easy to measure once they saw the large rectangle.

When they were beginning to problem-solve what to do with the trapezoids, one student thought about cutting squares to fill those triangles. If the other student hadn't blurted out to flip one trapezoid to make the rectangle, a fraction (*Curriculum Standard 12*) lesson may have begun.

They had many opportunities to collect data (*Curriculum Standard 11*). At first they had to talk about and decide what kind of house to build, as well as the site of the house. They collected data again when they had to decide on the color. This time, graphing was involved. By writing their color preference, then gluing it to construction paper, they were able to compare the results. With a large bar graph on the wall they could see what color the house would be painted.

The students used calculators to explore whole number operations (*Curriculum Standards 7* and *8*). They had to determine, in square feet, the size of the house. Then, they used the calculators to find out just how much paint they would need to cover the house. They considered what 1 quart would cover, as well as how much 1 gallon of paint would cover. As they thought about this relationship they were building on their sense of number (*Curriculum Standard 6*). They discovered if they doubled or tripled the amount of paint they could double or triple the amount of times they could paint the house.

There is a widespread feeling of accomplishment in Mrs. Hibbitts classroom. J.D. has a permanent house and it is all because of the efforts of the children (and Mrs. Hibbitts). Mrs. Hibbits spent an enormous amount of time preparing the environment for this unit. She set many goals and objectives, insuring that the tasks would be worthwhile (*Professional Standard 1*). She guided the classroom discussions in such a way that made students provide the questions and information.

It is the way questions are posed that directs discussion in a classroom. Mrs. Hibbits consistently engaged students in discussion (*Professional Standard 2*). She could have easily called her friend and asked him to build a house for J.D. but instead wanted the students to discuss J.D.'s needs and realize there was something they could do to help the bear.

Her questions often led to debate among the students. They often exchanged ideas and made conjectures (*Professional Standard 3*). Sometimes students' conjectures needed some prodding, so Mrs. Hibbits deliberated whether to use floor tiles or wall tiles for the measurement. What she really wanted was for someone to see that there might be a better way to measure. Again, Mrs. Hibbits could have just gotten out rulers and taught them about measuring in inches. Instead, she wanted them to use some nonstandard form of measurement, then transfer that notion to the standard form of inches.

She provided students with many tools for learning (*Professional Standard 4*). They began by looking at the tiles as a unit of measurement and then realized they could use tape measures. She gave them paper and pencil to draw their conceptions of J.D.'s house. The comparisons of their drawings brought about debate on what kind of house would be best. The graphing of color preference also brought about discussion; they had a visual (the bar graph) as the focus of discussion. More often than not, some form of debate or discussion was taking place in Mrs. Hibbitts classroom.

The students and J.D. had a wonderful, comfortable learning environment (*Professional Standard 5*) thanks to Mrs. Hibbits. She provided an environment that helped the students develop their mathematical skills. They were active, they were talkative, they were full of ideas. Mrs. Hibbitts evoked thought and promoted discussion. She believed in her students and held high expectations of their performance.

Her assessment (*Professional Standard 6*), as she said, was ongoing. Her assessment was not just on students' accomplishments, but also of her own performance. At the end of each activity, she considered how the lesson progressed, what she would need to think about for the following day, and what students' needs would be addressed the next day. Her objectives constantly reflected the

Mathematics Standard. The problems reflected real-life situations and enabled students to reason and communicate about mathematics.

Not only did she listen and observe, she was also careful to keep written records of students' comments and questions. She provided the students with small books in which they could record reflections and information. The students constantly connected mathematical ideas; they made connections between concepts, but also made connections to a real-life situation. Mrs. Hibbitts' assessment did reflect the mathematics that all students should know.

Students were also spotlighted for their uniqueness, as in the *Equity Standard.* They all brought in ideas and tried to find ways to make the ideas fit into the planning stage. Mrs. Hibbitts made notes of those ideas which were useful in her assessment of the students.

Although all the information may have been gathered before discussion began and building the house wasn't originally the children's idea, Mrs. Hibbitts had a way of empowering the students. Ultimately, it was the children's idea to build a house — and they did it quite well, as can be seen anytime if you walk into Marcia Hibbitts classroom!

This may not be the typical mathematics unit for an elementary curriculum, but it is an excellent example of what should be included in a unit. Teacher preparation should top the list. By considering the questions first, the teacher will be able to guide the students in the appropriate direction. By having materials ready, for example, paper and pencil for writing color preferences and paper and masking tape for designing the house, the teacher can enjoy the experience with the students. Mrs. Hibbitts is the kind of teacher who makes it all look so easy — strong preparation is what makes it look easy.

CONTACT

Marcia Hibbitts
John Foster Dulles Elementary
6481 Bridgetown Road
Cincinnati, OH 45248

4

COMMON CHARACTERISTICS

Whether teaching a few years or having recently retired, the educators described in these profiles share some common characteristics. They share an enthusiasm for teaching — they are all happy in their environment and value interactions with their students. They look forward to their work each day. In some cases, the educators were sought out by university faculty or state agencies to participate in research projects, in others the educators went looking for answers, ways to make change. They have all made changes; all have made a shift from a traditional approach to a more innovative approach to teaching, an approach that empowers students.

The enthusiasm that these teachers share must flow out to the students. It would seem that eager, enthusiastic teachers breed eager, enthusiastic students. The students in these profiles were not passive learners in the classroom, instead they were active participants in classroom activities.

The activities described in the profiles took time and energy on the part of the educators. An observer could walk into any of the classrooms described and see students working and talking, teachers listening and observing. To an observer, the job may look effortless, but a great deal of preparation time is involved — and that time is unobservable.

An equally important aspect of making these classrooms work was commitment. These educators were committed to making their ideas work, to implementing those ideas into the curriculum, to involving students in the learning process. This commitment drove their motivation.

REVISITING QUESTIONS

In Chapter 1, some questions were posed: "If children are to learn mathematics, what will they need to do?" and "What will teachers need to do?" Children will need to be involved in tasks and engaged in learning as opposed to being required to cover a certain number of pages by the end of a school year. In the profiles, the children were engaged in thought, discussion, and activity — they were learning mathematics.

Students were given problems to solve. In some cases, they were given real-life dilemmas. The dilemmas were of interest to them and they were eager to work; they wanted to solve problems. They wanted to build the house for J.D. They wanted to redesign their playground. They wanted to estimate then discover just how many seeds were in that watermelon. They wanted to roll the dice and decide where to put the numbers on the grid. They wanted to clap and sing to learn a new rhyme.

The classroom interactions played an important role in student learning. The interactions gave students a chance to listen to themselves think as well as listen to their peers. Lampert (1990) calls this kind of interaction "public construction." While students are making sense of information and thinking out loud, the teacher acts as a mediator to the discussion. The teacher listens but also guides students and challenges them to go beyond a factual explanation. As students react to and reflect on the discussion, they are constructing knowledge, they are learning mathematics.

If we want students to learn mathematics, then our (the teachers') goals should be to create and foster problem-solving situations in the classroom, provide an arena for students to react to and reflect on discussion, and ensure that students feel secure and comfortable enough to verbally reflect on ideas.

We did not provide examples of teachers saying, "Now, let's turn to page 25." Students did not moan and groan when it was time to measure the walls for J.D.'s house or play "roll a problem." There was a predictable unpredictability about some of these classrooms. There was always something going on, some new question the teacher might ask, some reason for the students to sit on the edge of their seats waiting to see what would come next! When students are told day after day to turn to a particular page in the text, they grow bored very quickly — they don't look forward to the next lesson, the next day.

When teachers create and foster problem-solving situations students feel challenged. The conflict requires thought, and conflict is a necessary component of knowledge construction (Ginsburg & Opper, 1988). The conflict is what triggers the sense-making process in which children actively monitor and adjust their thinking.

It is often through classroom discussion that conflicting points of view are resolved. The sense-making process continues as children listen, compare, and contrast points of view. It is the teacher's role to act as ". . . mediator between students' thinking and mathematical conventions" (Lampert, 1990, p. 254). There may be times that the teacher will say little more than, "Are there any other ideas?" or "Keep going . . . ," while other times the teacher may need to help students clarify their thoughts or positions. These actions will help the students react to and reflect on the discussion.

When a teacher lets students know their ideas matter, that their comments are accepted, the environment becomes secure and favorable for discussion (Lampert, 1990). The students must feel they are in a safe environment before they are able to take risks, to talk about their reflections (Wood, Cobb, & Yackel, 1991). To create this environment, the teacher must convey the notion that all answers (mistakes included) are acceptable, even encouraged. The teacher must listen to the students' questions and answers; listening lets them know that what they say has some value. The students will become more willing to discuss their viewpoints when this environment is created.

The third question in the first chapter asked: "What should the study of mathematics entail?" The profiles in this book are just the beginning of the descriptions of what the study of mathematics should entail. Based on the profiles and the *Curriculum and Evaluation Standards* it appears that the study of mathematics should be looked at more holistically. Concepts cannot be taught as a series of isolated facts. "Mr. Goodmath" focused on the operation of addition in the videotape we viewed, but he showed a variety of approaches to the operation. Ms. Anderson taught students some songs and rhymes, but it was only after spending time on concepts and gaining understanding of the concepts. Ms. Smith asked general questions that could fit into any lesson. Ms. Foote integrated mathematics into every part of her school day.

When students built the house for J.D. or redesigned the play-ground, they used every mathematical concept mentioned in the *Standards*. When students are exposed to literature that provides them with some history of their culture, they are making connections, the concepts have some meaning. When students are required to talk to family members and classmates about budgeting money they are discerning valid reasons for learning mathematics.

CREATING AN AUTONOMOUS ENVIRONMENT

Posing problems and playing games is not enough to enthuse students or make the classroom run smoothly. What is needed is what was found in these profiles. The underlying current in the classrooms described was the presence of an autonomous environ-ment. The educators delegated responsibility to the students. In other words, the adult was not the authority, everyone shared equal-ly in the work and in the discussion. Students built self-esteem and self-respect; they believed they had some control in the classroom. They felt that their ideas were important, that there was some value to what they had to say. They were given the freedom to explore their thoughts and ideas.

When considering an autonomous environment, one concern for teachers becomes behavior problems. Giving students responsi-bility and control can be a monumental task. Teachers may try a "new method" of teaching, but if students are not attending and are "acting up," the traditional ways of teaching can quietly return (von Glasersfeld, 1990). Teachers often teach based on their own experiences as students; in other words, they teach the way they were taught (Lortie, 1975). Therefore, if a new method does not feel comfortable to a teacher, that teacher may revert back to the more traditional methods of teaching.

Interestingly, there were no real behavior problems in these classrooms — and some of the educators had quite a range, in terms of student abilities and grade levels, in their classrooms. A common comment was, if the children are involved in the lesson, if they are interacting with problems, with the environment, with each other, then behavior is not a problem. If children are involved, if they have been given worthwhile tasks, then they come to know that the teacher is truly interested in their work. That self-worth builds the intrinsic motivation to work. Also, they are so involved and so busy with their work that they don't even consider misbehaving.

What must be built into any teacher's thoughts on creating an autonomous environment is trust. The teacher must trust that, with time, as the teacher finds the appropriate activities for students they will become engaged in the activities. As students become interested and engaged, behaviors cease to be a problem. If the teacher acquires or creates worthwhile mathematical tasks, then students will not question the task but will instead jump right in to solve the problem.

If an autonomous environment is not created, then it will be impossible to incorporate the *Standards* into instruction. If the teacher has all the "right answers," what is the point of problem-solving? The teacher takes away the students' motivation when he/she has all the answers.

WHAT CAN A CLASSROOM TEACHER DO?

How can these profiles help? The answer can be divided into three sections. Teachers should actively involve children in the learning process by providing them with problems to solve, teachers should provide children with time and opportunity to think and talk about the problems given, and teachers should provide a comfortable, secure environment conducive to students feeling free to take risks.

The problems teacher provide must be of interest to the children. *Professional Standard 1* recounts the importance of creating worthwhile mathematical tasks. If a teacher can uncover students' interests and dilemmas then he/she will be better able to create problem situations. Uncovering their interests as well as dilemmas will take keen observation skills.

The teacher can always begin by conducting an informal survey (verbal or written) or an interest inventory. The survey or inventory can reveal likes and dislikes, hobbies, or favorite foods and television shows. The teacher can use these ideas to pose problems to the class. The teacher can look at the word problems in the mathematics textbook and change the words in such a way to make it more interesting and believable to the students: use the students names, their hobbies, their favorite television shows.

Observation may be the only way to find out about dilemmas. Mrs. Hibbitts discovered, with her students, how important it was to find a home for J.D. Ms. Wetjen realized, as students were getting into trouble at recess, that they needed help with their playground. Ms. Anderson knew that her students understood basic mathematics facts, but that they were having trouble memorizing them, so she wrote songs for them. Observation is ongoing. It is one way to find out what children know and what they need to know as well as what the classroom teacher is doing and what might need to be done differently (*Professional Standard 6: Analysis of Teaching and Learning*).

Deciding what to do with the observed information may be a dilemma in itself. The teacher must decide, once he/she has this information, what to do with it. Mrs. Hibbitts took her time. Once she realized they needed a house for J.D. she took the time to think and research the idea. The playground issue was not resolved overnight. Being well-planned and well-organized will greatly benefit any project or problem to be solved.

It can be difficult for a teacher to give students time to think about and talk about problems. When a teacher sees a student sitting at a table baffled over a problem, a first instinct may be to tell the student what to do. By giving students answers and telling them what to do, teachers are conveying the message that they are mainly interested in getting an answer.

If given time to think, Kamii and Joseph (1989) believe children will construct their own knowledge and ultimately arrive at the correct answer. They will come to understand mathematical concepts as they make sense of information and as they listen to themselves and others (Yackel, Cobb, Wood, Wheatley, & Merkel, 1990). "Mathematical knowledge cannot be given to children" (p. 13). As tempting as it may be to tell children how to "do it," the only way for them to come to understand is to provide them with the problem and give them time to think about the problem.

Children will also need time to talk about the problem. There are different ways to provide time to think out loud. The teacher can call on students, one at a time; of course, there may not be time for everyone to talk. If the students have been working in small groups, they should all have the opportunity to talk. The teacher can also tell the students to turn to neighbors to talk about what they know. If students are given the opportunity to talk, to verbally reflect on their ideas then the teacher has been successful with the public construction of knowledge — success will depend on the teacher's listening and observing as students think out loud.

The secure environment cannot be stressed enough. Without this kind of environment, mathematical understanding may be limited. If students are afraid to talk about their thinking, or afraid to provide an answer because it may sound "silly," then verbal reflection will be restricted. The reflection on mental and physical actions is key to creating mathematical knowledge (Clements & Battista (1990). If children don't feel comfortable enough to say what they are thinking, what does that say for their construction of mathematical knowledge?

The creation of this environment may take time. It will be dependent upon students' experiences in other classrooms — experiences with previous teachers may cloud the creation of the environment. We, as well as many of you, have stories of experiencing great humiliation in an elementary classroom. Humiliation will stunt any student's learning potential; no longer will he/she be willing to speak up, to tell the class what he/she is thinking.

CONCLUSION

We hope you will take information from these profiles and use the information in the classroom. Experiment to find out what parts of the profiles will work for you. The educators described in the profiles didn't just stumble into something fun and worthwhile, they spent time considering ideas and getting to know their students. They spent time reading books. They listened to other teachers to find out what was working in other classrooms. The listened to students in order to gather information on students' interests.

The educators described in the profiles are dedicated and committed to providing worthwhile mathematical tasks that engage all of their students. It is hoped that other teachers will provide tasks based on students' experiences and interests. It is through these tasks, that teachers will need to guide students to make connections between mathematical topics as well as real-life situations around them. If students can make connections between real-life experiences and the mathematics they are learning they will no longer ask, "Why do we need to know this?"

APPENDIX A

NAMES AND ADDRESSES OF PROFILED EDUCATORS

Altieri, Mary
Van Cortlandtville Elementary School
Main Street
Mohegan Lake, NY 10547

Anderson, Marilyn
T.C. Cherry Elementary School
1001 Liberty Avenue
Bowling Green, KY 42104

Boggs, Beverly
Circleville School
PO Box 9
Circleville, WV 26804

Buehler, Deb
San Antonio Zoo
3903 N. St. Mary's Street
San Antonio, TX 78212

Diener, Kristine
School District of Waukesha
222 Maple Avenue
Waukesha, WI 53186

Foote, Mary
PS 84
32 W. 92nd Street
New York, NY 10025

Garza, Korine
Southmost Elementary School
5245 Southmost Road
Brownsville, TX 78521

Hibbitts, Marcia
John Foster Dulles Elementary
6481 Bridgetown Road
Cincinnati, OH 45248

LaGrone, Jean
Westgate Elementary School
7802 Hascall
Omaha, NE 68124

Messenger, Deborah
Indianapolis Zoological Society, Inc.
1200 W. Washington Street
Indianapolis, IN 46222

Moseley, Lois
Region IV Education Service Center
7145 West Tidwell
Houston, TX 77092

Rooney, Mike
Welleby Elementary School
3230 Nob Hill Road
Sunrise, Florida, 33351

Smith, Priscilla
Kingsley School
2300 Green Bay Road
Evanston, Illinois, 60201

Fraivillig, Judith
email: fraivillig@columbia.edu

Wetjen, Dianne
1690 Rainbow Court
Marco Island, FL 33937

APPENDIX B

SUGGESTED READINGS

Carpenter, T.P. (1985). Learning to add and subtract: An exercise in problem solving. In E.A. Silver (Ed.), *Teaching and learning mathematical problem solving: Multiple research perspectives* (pp. 17–40). Hillsdale, NJ: Lawrence Erlbaum Associates, Inc.

Clements, D.H., & Battista, M.T. (1990). Constructivist learning and teaching. *Arithmetic Teacher, 38*(1), 34–35.

Fraivillig, J. (1995). Advancing children's mathematical thinking: A case study of an expert teacher. (Paper presented at the Annual Meeting of the American Educational Research Association, April, 1995, San Francisco, CA.) Washington, DC: National Science Foundation, Grant No. ESI 9252984.

Ginsburg, H., & Opper, S. (1988). Learning, development, and education. *Piaget's theory of intellectual development* (pp. 208-256). New Jersey: Prentice Hall.

Kamii, C., & Joseph, L. (1989). *Young children continue to reinvent arithmetic — 2nd grade — Implications of Piaget's theory.* New York: Teachers College Press.

Lampert, M. (1990). Connecting inventions with conventions. In L. Steffe & T. Wood (Eds.), *Transforming children's mathematics education* (pp. 253–265). Hillsdale, NJ: Lawrence Erlbaum Associates, Inc.

Lortie, D.C. (1975). Speculations on change. *Schoolteacher* (pp. 214–244). Chicago: The University of Chicago Press.

National Council of Teachers of Mathematics. (1989). *Curriculum and evaluation standards for school mathematics.* Reston, VA: NCTM, Inc.

National Council of Teachers of Mathematics. (1991). *Professional standards for teaching mathematics.* Reston, VA: NCTM, Inc.

National Council of Teachers of Mathematics. (1995). *Assessment standards for school mathematics*. Reston, VA: NCTM, Inc.

Peterson, P., Fennema, E., Carpenter, T., & Loef, M. (1989). Teachers' pedagogical content beliefs in mathematics. *Cognition and Instruction, 6*(1), 1–40.

Resnick, L. (1987). *Education and learning to think*. Washington, DC: National Academy Press.

Schifter, D., & Fosnot, C. (1993). *Reconstructing mathematics education*. New York: Teachers College Press.

Silverstein, S. (1974). *Where the Sidewalk Ends*. New York: Harper & Row.

von Glasersfeld, E. (1990). An exposition of constructivism: Why some like it radical. In R.B. Davis, C.A. Maher, & N. Noddings (Eds.), *Constructivist views on the teaching and learning of mathematics* (Journal for Research in Mathematics Education, Monograph No. 4). (pp. 19-29). Reston, Virginia: NCTM, Inc.

Wood, T., Cobb, P., & Yackel, E. (1991). Change in teaching mathematics: A case study. *American Educational Research Journal, 28*(3), 587–616.

Yackel, E., Cobb, P., Wood, T., & Merkel, G. (1990). Experience, problem solving, and discourse as central aspects of constructivism. *Arithmetic Teacher, 38*(4), 34–35.

Yackel, E., Cobb, P., Wood, T., Wheatley, G., & Merkel, G. (1990). The importance of social interaction in children's construction of mathematical knowledge. In T.J. Cooney & C.R. Hirsch (Eds.), *Teaching and Learning Mathematics in the 1990s* (pp. 12–21). Reston, VA: NCTM, Inc.

DATE DUE

2301			